¡Ya!

Activity Book 1

Curso de español

Ulla Håkanson
Joaquín Masoliver
Gunilla Sandström

Adapted by
Hedley Sharples

Oxford University Press

Oxford University Press, Walton Street, Oxford OX2 6DP

Oxford   New York
Athens   Auckland   Bangkok   Bombay
Calcutta   Cape Town   Dar es Salaam   Delhi
Florence   Hong Kong   Istanbul   Karachi
Kuala Lumpur   Madras   Madrid   Melbourne
Mexico City   Nairobi   Paris   Singapore
Taipei   Tokyo   Toronto

and associated companies in
Berlin   Ibadan

Oxford is a trade mark of Oxford University Press

Originally published by Almqvist & Wiksell under the title
Eso sí 1

© 1983 Ulla Håkanson, Joaquín Masoliver, Gunilla
Sandström, Hans L. Beeck and Almqvist & Wiksell
Läromedel AB, Stockholm

© This edition: Oxford University Press 1984
ISBN 0 19 912055 2

First published 1984
Reprinted 1985, 1987, 1988, 1990, 1991, 1992, 1993, 1995

Acknowledgements

Translated from the Swedish by Joan Tate.

Illustrations are by Göran Schultz.

The publishers would like to thank the following for
permission to reproduce photographs:
Bildagenturen   *67*
Peter Kjellerås/MIRAS   *96*
Klaesson/Olsson/Bildhuset   *51(1)*
Wolf Krabel   *18*
Nils-Johan Norenlind   *95*
Maud Nycander/MIRA   *51(2), 66, 85*
Sven Oredson/Bildhuset   *60*
Ulrika Palme   *65*
Scandibild/A.G.E.   *98*
Svenskt Pressfoto   *62*

Copyright List

Map of Spain in Roman times from Esselete Studium,
Atlas of World History, © Esselte Studium, Stockholm   *31*

'El primer resfriado' by Celia Vinas Olivella, from *Poesía
española para niños*, © Taurus Ediciones, S.A.,
Madrid   *63*

'Es la clase . . .' by Antonio Machado, from *Poesías*,
© Editorial Losada, S.A., Buenos Aires   *91*

'Elena y María' by C.J. Cela, from *Viaje a la Alcarria*,
© Espasa Calpa, S.A., Madrid   *97*

'El egoísta' by Pablo Neruda, © Editorial Losada, S.A.,
Buenos Aires   *97*

'La lluvia', anonymous author, from *Poesía española para
niños*, © Taurus Ediciones, S.A., Madrid   *97*

'El sol', anonymous author, from *Poesía española para niños*,
© Taurus Ediciones, S.A., Madrid   *97*

Phototypeset by Tradespools Limited, Frome, Somerset

Printed in Hong Kong

Contents

Introduction *3*
Exercises and information, units 1–42 *5–88*
Si tiene tiempo *89*
Unit vocabularies *99*
Supplement to certain exercises *119*
English-Spanish vocabulary *123*

Introduction

¡Ya! 1 Students' Book contains a number of exercises linked to the texts, including questions, summaries, listening exercises, dialogues, and descriptions of pictures.

¡Ya! 1 Activity Book also contains examples of these types of exercise, plus a wide variety of other activities. These include role-play, interviews, gap-filling exercises, pronunciation and intonation exercises, translations, vocabulary building, reading comprehension, and practice in both situational dialogues and conversation.

Apart from the exercises, the Activity Book contains:

- *background information panels* in English, inserted among the exercises
- additional sections entitled *Si tiene tiempo* ('If you have time')
- *unit vocabularies* which refer to the texts in the Students' Book
- an *English-Spanish vocabulary*

How to use the exercises

There are many exercises in **¡Ya! 1** for the student who wishes to work individually, but as it is very useful to listen to one another, it is hoped that you will often work in pairs, and learn from each other.

Remember to practise each exercise thoroughly. It is not enough simply to find the answer. Practise so that each conversation flows well. It is better to do fewer exercises and do them well. What you have practised thoroughly will be what you remember later.

Keep a balance between oral and written work. Certain exercises are more suitable as written exercises (e.g. translation and descriptions of pictures), but with other exercises too (e.g. asking questions, interviews, conversations), it is sometimes best to write them down first, then correct them and, finally, practise them – or to practise them orally first, and then write them down.

Students work at varying paces, and not every student will want to do every exercise. It is easy to choose from the exercises in ¡Ya!, as every exercise has a clear heading and, where appropriate, a reference to the grammar section in the Students' Book.

Make sure that you do different types of exercise. Even if you do not have time to do all the exercises, you should find time to do some of the freer exercises. You will soon discover that you can cope with many situations in Spanish.

Remember to look in the Activity Book to see the order in which the exercises come.

The exercise in the Students' Book is not necessarily the one to be done first.

Before each exercise, the earliest stage at which it can be used is stated, but many exercises, such as sentence-building, translation or descriptions of pictures, do not have to be done while you are working on that particular unit. Don't stop because you have not had time to do them. Continue with the next unit and use the unused exercises as revision, or as homework.

The exercises can be used for testing. You should be able to do most of the exercises without help. If this is not so, then you probably need to go back and revise.

There are a great many illustrations in the Activity Book – photographs, drawings, maps, etc. Use them! Illustrations are an invaluable aid to learning a language.

We hope that whether you are learning Spanish at school, in adult education, in study groups or on your own, you will find ¡Ya! stimulating to work with.

Good luck!

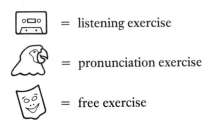

= listening exercise

= pronunciation exercise

= free exercise

1 América Latina · Europa

 A Pronunciación

Escuche la cinta y repita. *Listen to the tape and repeat.*

Chile	**ch**	Canarias	**c [k]**	Barcelona	**b, v**
España	**ñ**	Colombia		Valencia	
Mallorca	**ll**	Cuba		La Habana	
Perú	**r**	Océano Pacífico	**c [θ]**	Montevideo	
Andorra	**rr**	Galicia	**g [g]**	Dinamarca	**d**
Honduras	**h**	Gomera		Granada	
San José	**j**	Guatemala		Madrid	
Quito	**qu**	Argentina	**g [χ]**	Extremadura	**x**
La Paz	**z**	Gibraltar			

Spanish vowels are all short. There is more information on pronunciation and spelling in ¶ 81–89.

B El alfabeto español

avión · bolso · cinco · chico · disco · elefante · fábrica · gato · helado · iglesia · jarra · kilo · libro · llave · mesa · naranja · señor · ojo · perro · queso · radio · silla · taza · uno · vaso · taxi · yogur · zapato

2 En el aeropuerto

After dialogue 1

A Numbers 1–10 · ¶ 14

Pregunte y conteste como en el ejemplo.
Ask the question and answer as in the example.

– El avión para Roma,
  ¿ qué puerta es, por favor?
o Puerta número 6.

SALIDAS	PUERTA
ROMA	6 ○
BARCELONA	1 ○
LISBOA	7 ○
PARIS	9 ○
BUENOS AIRES	10 ○
COPENHAGUE	3 ○
LONDRES	4 ○
HAMBURGO	8 ○
MALAGA	2 ○

22:00

Barajas, the airport for Madrid, is 13 kilometres from the centre of the city. In number of passengers, Barajas is the fifth largest airport in Europe.

After dialogue 3

B Greetings

1 Complete el diálogo. *Fill in the dialogue.*

– Buenos días, señorita.
o ¹.................., señora. ¿ Cómo ².................. usted?
– Muy ³.................., gracias. ¿ Y ⁴..................?
o Bien, ⁵...................

2 Make up a similar dialogue using **tú**.

After p. 7

C Rellene la tarjeta

Fill in this card

TARJETA DE ENTRADA/SALIDA
ENTRY/EXIT CARD

Apellidos
Surname
Nom ....

Nombre
Name
Prénom ....

Profesión
Profession
Profession ....

Domicilio
Domicile
Domicile ....

País
Country
Pays ....

Pasaporte n⁰
Passport
Passeport ....

Lugar emisión
Place of issue
Lieu d'émission ....

student –
estudiante

Spaniards have two surnames, the father's and the mother's. When a woman marries, she keeps her father's surname and then adds (usually with **de** in front of it) her husband's first surname. If María González Salas marries Antonio Rodríguez Gallardo, she becomes María González (de) Rodríguez. In everyday speech however, one surname only tends to be used, and when signing a document, a woman uses her parents' surnames.

D Presentación

Tell each other where you are from and what your name is. Introduce yourselves and your friends to the teacher.

E Pronunciación *r, rr* · ¶ 83

r Francia Perú Ecuador
rr Herrera Inglaterra Mediterráneo
Marruecos República Dominicana

3 En la aduana

After dialogue 1

A Indefinite article · ¶ 1

Conteste como en el ejemplo. *Answer as in the example.*

1 – ¿ Qué es esto?
   ○ Es un libro.

4 – ¿ Qué es esto?
   ○ ....

2 – ¿ Qué es esto?
   ○ ....

5 – ¿ Qué es esto?
   ○ ....

3 – ¿ Qué es esto?
   ○ ....

After dialogue 2

B Definite and indefinite article · ¶ 1

Pregunte y conteste como en el ejemplo. *Ask the question and answer as in the example.*

1 – ¿ Qué hay en el bolso?
   ○ Hay un libro y una revista.

2 – ¿ Qué hay en .... ?
   ○ ....

3 – ¿ Qué hay en la maleta?
   ○ ....

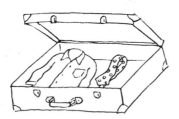

4 – ¿ Qué hay en .... ?
   ○ ....

C Plural · ¶ 5 B

Lea como en el ejemplo. *Read as in the example.*

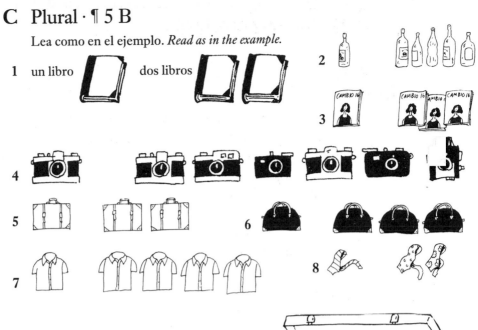

1 un libro   dos libros

2

3

4

5   6

7   8

D Construya dos diálogos.

Make up two dialogues using the pictures.

– ¿ Qué hay en la maleta?
○ ¿ En qué maleta?
○ En la maleta ....

○ Hay ① ....
– ¿ Algo más?
○ Sí, hay también ② ....

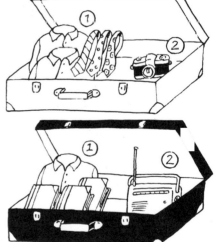

After dialogue 3

E ¿Cuántos? ¿Cuántas? · ¶ 32

Pregunte y conteste como en el ejemplo.

1 – ¿Cuántos libros hay en el bolso?   3 – ¿ .... ?
   ○ Hay dos.   ○ ....

2 – ¿ .... ?
   ○ ....

4 – ¿ .... ?
   ○ ....

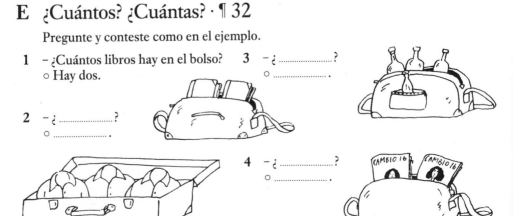

F Libro de textos, página 9

G En la aduana

Escriban el diálogo y representen la escena. *Write the dialogue and act out the scene.*

El aduanero *Customs officer*	**El viajero** *Traveller*
Ask for the traveller's passport.	
	Hand it over.
Ask for the traveller's name.	
	Give your name.
Ask what is in the suitcase.	
	Say what is in it (not bottles or cigarettes).
Ask if there is anything else.	
	Remember that there are also some bottles.
Ask how many.	
	Say that there are three.
Ask if there are also cigarettes in the suitcase.	
	Say yes.
Ask how many packets.	
	Say how many (10 at the most).
Say that's all right.	
	Say thank you.

Tú or **usted**?
The use of **tú** (you, informal) is becoming more usual in Spain today, but in shops, hotels, and other service establishments, **usted** (you, formal) is used.

4 España

A   Libro de textos, página 10 ('Substitute . . .')

After p. 10

B   *No* + verb · ¶ 76 A

Mire el mapa de la página cuatro del libro de textos.
Look at the map on p. 4 of the Students' Book.

Pregunte y conteste como en el ejemplo.

1   – ¿Lima está también en <u>España</u>?
    ○ No, Lima no está en Espana.
     Está en Perú.
2   Caracas – Perú – ¿?
3   Quito – Venezuela – ¿?
4   Santiago – Ecuador – ¿?

5   La Habana – Chile – ¿?
6   Bogotá – Cuba – ¿?
7   Buenos Aires – Colombia – ¿?
8   Asunción – Argentina – ¿?
9   Montevideo – Paraguay – ¿?
10   La Paz – Uruguay – ¿?

After p. 11

C   Libro de textos, página 11 ('Conteste a las preguntas.')

> **Castellano** was originally the language spoken by the inhabitants of Castilla la Nueva and Castilla la Vieja in central Spain. Today **castellano** is synonymous with **español**, and both mean the Spanish language.
> *Note* In certain Spanish-speaking countries in America, the word **español** is used when referring to the Spanish spoken in Spain, whereas **castellano** is used to mean the Spanish language in general.

D   Traduzca al español.

Translate into Spanish.

At the airport
– I'm from Edinburgh. And you?
○ From Maracaibo.
– What country is that in?
○ In Venezuela.
– Is Caracas in Venezuela too?
○ Yes, in the north, on the coast.

E   ¿Con qué países limita?

Mire el mapa de la página cuatro del libro de textos.
Look at the map on p. 4 of the Students' Book.

Conteste a las preguntas.
¿Con qué países limita. . . ?

1   Colombia
2   Perú

3   Argentina
4   Bolivia

F Escuche.

1 Escuche la cinta y rellene el texto.
Listen to the tape and fill in the gaps.

[1]_____ está [2]_____ América [3]_____.

Aquí se habla [4]_____. Además se hablan otras

[5]_____, por ejemplo el mapuche.

[6]_____ se llama Santiago.

Está en [7]_____ del país.

Antofagasta está [8]_____,

Punta Arenas [9]_____.

Estas ciudades están [10]_____
del Océano Pacífico.

[11]_____
Perú, Bolivia y Argentina.

2 Copy the map and write in the names.

G Colombia

Mire el mapa y lea el texto.

Barranquilla ●
PANAMÁ   VENEZUELA
● Medellín
■ Bogotá
● COLOMBIA
Popayán
ECUADOR   BRASIL
PERÚ

BOLIVIA PARAGUAY
● Tucumán
ARGENTINA   BRASIL
Córdoba
URUGUAY
● Mendoza
Buenos Aires ■
● Mar del Plata
CHILE

Esto es Colombia. Aquí se habla español.
Bogotá es la capital de Colombia. Está en el
centro del país. Barranquilla es una ciudad grande.
Está en el norte. Medellín está en el oeste,
Popayán en el sur. Colombia limita con Panamá,
Venezuela, Brasil, Perú y Ecuador.

H Escriba un texto.

Write some sentences as in G about:

1 Argentina   **2** your own country   (Inglaterra – *England*; inglés – *English*)

5 Al centro

After p. 12

A A la, al · ¶ 1 D

Pedro, Laura y las otras personas están en el aeropuerto.
¿Adónde van?   *Where are they going?*
Rellene los letreros.   *Fill in the boxes in Spanish.*
Pregunte y conteste como en el ejemplo.

1 – ¿Adónde va <u>el señor Aldana</u>?   4 el señor López
  ○ Va a la parada de autobús.   5 la señora Peralta
2 Laura   6 la señorita Gómez
3 Pedro   7 la señora Pérez

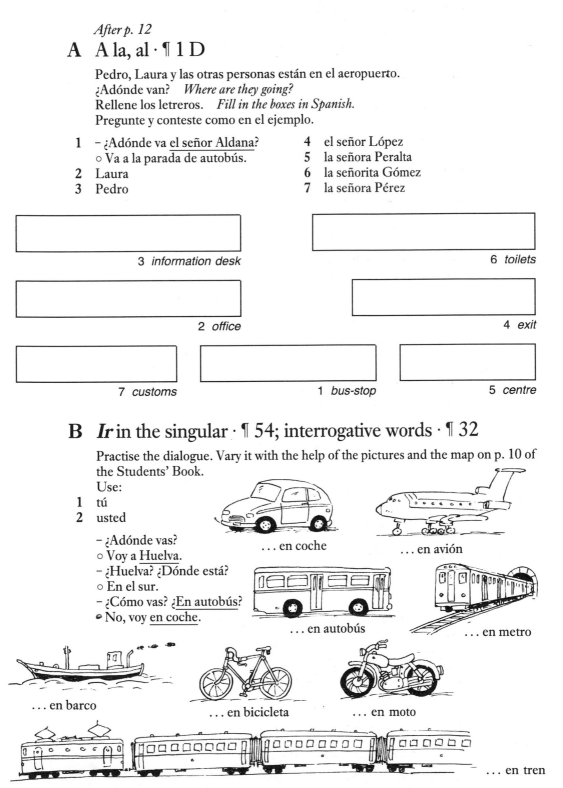

3 *information desk*	6 *toilets*
2 *office*	4 *exit*
7 *customs* 1 *bus-stop*	5 *centre*

B *Ir* in the singular · ¶ 54; interrogative words · ¶ 32

Practise the dialogue. Vary it with the help of the pictures and the map on p. 10 of
the Students' Book.
Use:
1 tú
2 usted

– ¿Adónde vas?
○ Voy a Huelva.
– ¿Huelva? ¿Dónde está?
○ En el sur.
– ¿Cómo vas? <u>¿En autobús?</u>
☛ No, voy <u>en coche</u>.

. . . en coche

. . . en avión

. . . en autobús

. . . en metro

. . . en barco

. . . en bicicleta

. . . en moto

. . . en tren

13

C En la calle

Escriba un diálogo entre las personas A y B.
Write a dialogue between A and B, using **tú**.

A	B
Greet B.	
	Greet A. Ask how A is.
Say how you are. Ask how B is.	
	Say how you are. Ask where A is going.
Answer with the name of a Spanish town.	
	Repeat the name. Ask where it is.
Say where the town is (in the north, on the coast . . .).	
	Ask how A is going to get there.
Say which form of transport you have chosen.	
	Say goodbye.

Buenos días – said in the morning up to the midday meal, which is at about two o'clock.
Buenas tardes – said in the afternoon until nightfall.
Buenas noches – said after nightfall.

D Pronunciación *c, z* · ¶ 83 (Note *seseo* s p. 133, 135)

Lea:

En el centro de la ciudad de La Paz,
cerca de la Plaza de la Estación,
está la oficina de Mercedes García.

6 En el centro de la ciudad

After line 6

A Libro de textos, página 14 ('Conteste a las preguntas.')

B Indefinite article · ¶ 1

En el aeropuerto hay una oficina de objetos perdidos. ¿Qué hay allí?
Escriba el nombre de cada objeto (con artículo indefinido).
At the airport there is a lost-property office. What is in it? Write down the name of each object (with the indefinite article).

Objetos perdidos

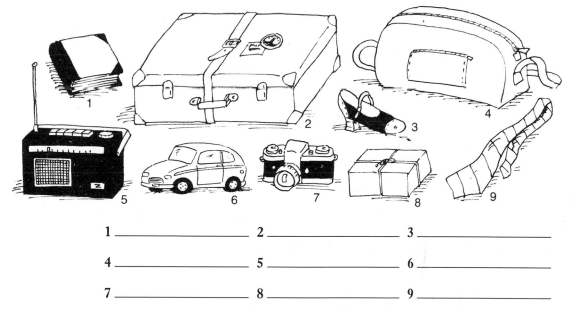

1 _____ 2 _____ 3 _____

4 _____ 5 _____ 6 _____

7 _____ 8 _____ 9 _____

C Definite and indefinite article · ¶ 1

¿el, un, la, una? Rellene con la forma correcta.

En la oficina de objetos perdidos hay ¹ _en la_ maleta negra.

En ² _la_ maleta hay ³_en el_ bolso grande.

En ⁴ _el_ bolso grande hay ⁵ _el_ bolso pequeño.

En el bolso pequeño hay ⁶_____ paquete.

En el paquete hay . . . (¿Qué hay? *Make up an answer yourself.*)

_____.

15

D Plural *-s, -es* · ¶ 5 B

Complete como en el ejemplo.

un avión – dos aviones
... autobús – dos ...
... coche –
... calle –
... bar –
... hotel –
... ciudad –
... pensión –
... restaurante –
... bolso –

After p. 14

E Pregunte y conteste. (1)

Pregunte y conteste como en el ejemplo.

– ¿Dónde está el hotel Cervantes, por favor?
○ No sé dónde está. Pregunte en el bar.

el hotel Cervantes	*el bar*
el restaurante Colón	el hotel
la terminal	la farmacia
la estación de Serrano	la información

After p. 15

F Pregunte y conteste. (2)

Pregunte y conteste como en el ejemplo.

– ¿Dónde está el hotel Goya, por favor?
○ Pues en la calle Goya.
– ¿ Está lejos?
○ No, allí, allí enfrente.
– Muchas gracias.
○ De nada.

el hotel Goya	*la calle Goya*
la terminal	la plaza de Colón
la estación de Serrano	la calle de Serrano
el Teatro Español	la plaza Santa Ana

G Libro de textos, página 15

H Traduzca al español.

Ana María is in the square. She is looking for a chemist's.
There is a stationer's on the corner. Ana María goes in.
She asks where there is a chemist's.
There is a chemist's in Montera Street.
It is nearby. Ana María goes there on foot.

I Conversación en la calle

Trabajen en grupos de tres.   *Work in groups of three.*

Two people (**A** and **B**) are standing talking on the pavement. A third (**C**) comes up to them to ask something. You are the three people and you carry on a conversation between you. Each of you has a section. Follow the numbers within the sections.

C
1   Ask politely where the Hotel León is.
6   Repeat the name of the street. Ask if it's nearby.
8   Say you're in a car.

A
2   Say that you don't know.
4   Say something that shows that you are disagreeing. The hotel there is called San Antonio.
7   Ask if C is on foot.

B
3   Say that it's in the Calle de León.
5   Say 'Of course, I'm sorry.' The Hotel León is in the Carrera de San Jerónimo.
9   Say that it's not far, near the parliament building.

near – cerca de
parliament building – Las Cortes (name of Parliament: Congreso de los Diputados)

7 La capital de España

After p. 16
A Definite article, plural · ¶ 1

Escriba con artículo definido.
Go back to 6D. Write down the words using the definite article.

el avión – los aviones

. . .

After p. 17
B Madrid

Say in Spanish what you know about Madrid.

C Caracas

This is a photo of Caracas. Write a few sentences about it. Start like this:
Caracas, con ..., está ...

La población de ...	
Madrid, provincia	4.726.986
Madrid, capital	3.158.818
España	37.380.826
Caracas, capital	4.479.000
Venezuela	15.284.000
	(cifras de 1980, 1981)

8 *Una individual sin ducha*

A Libro de textos, p. 18 ('Fill in Mr Aldana's reservation')

B Libro de textos, p. 18 ('Reserve una habitación.')

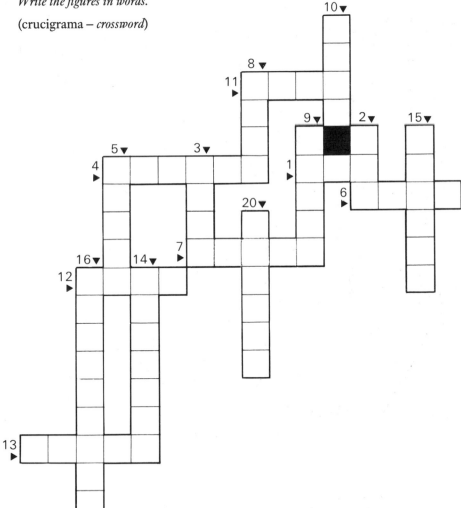 **C** Libro de textos, p. 18

D Crucigrama · ¶ 14 (numbers)

Escriba las cifras con letras.
Write the figures in words.

(crucigrama – *crossword*)

9 En casa de los Gómez

A Libro de textos, p. 20 ('Conteste a las preguntas.')

B Libro de textos, p. 21 ('Describa el comedor.')

C ¿Está o hay? · ¶ 33 A, C

1 Complete con la forma correcta.
Fill in the correct form of **está** *or* **hay**.

La familia de Mercedes ¹_____ en el comedor. Allí ²_____

una mesa. También ³_____ seis sillas. ⁴_____ además

un televisor. El televisor ⁵_____ en un rincón.

2 Give the rule for when you use *hay* and when *está/están*.

D El comedor de los Blanco

Escriba usted un texto corto sobre el comedor de la familia Blanco.
Write a few sentences about the Blanco family's dining-room.

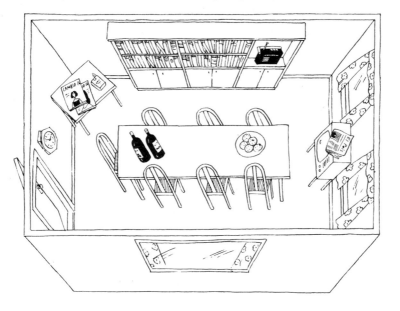

E Pronunciación *11, ch* · ¶ 83 (Note *yeísmo* p. 134)

Lea:

ll Allí en la silla amarilla
hay una botella y una tortilla.

ch Muchos chicos y chicas de Aluche
escuchan música chilena en la ducha.

10 Después de cenar...

After line 13

A Personal pronouns · ¶ 18 A

- What does *Necesitamos . . .* mean?
- Translate into Spanish:

1 I'm well.
2 How are you?
3 I'm from Madrid. And you?

4 Carmen and her father are going.
5 Her father is going by train, but she is going by car.

- Which form did you use for the personal pronouns? (If you need to know what the other personal pronouns are in Spanish, look them up in ¶ 18.)

B Verbos en *-ar* · ¶ 34 A

Write down all the forms of the present tense of the *-ar* verbs in the text (lines 1–13) in unit 10. What are their infinitives? What are they in English?

C Entrevista muy corta

Trabajen de dos en dos.

Each of you take a part in this brief interview with Mercedes Gómez, one translating the questions into Spanish, the other preparing to play the part of Mercedes. (Units 8–10)

Questions (use *usted*):

1 What's your name?
2 Where do you work?
3 What's it called?
4 Where is it?
5 What's your sister's name?

6 Does she work at the boarding-house too?
7 Why is she looking for another job?

entrevista (f) – *interview*
corto, -a – *short*

Ofertas de empleo

D ¿Por qué? – Porque . . . · ¶ 32

Pregunte y conteste como en el ejemplo.

1 – ¿Por qué compra Mercedes el periódico de la tarde?
○ Porque buscan otro trabajo para Clara.

2 (Clara busca otro trabajo.)
(Es muy aburrido estar en la caja todo el día.)

3 (Las chicas miran en El País.)
(Allí también hay anuncios.)

4 (Pablo trabaja en una compañía norteamericana.)
(Desea ganar más dinero.)

5 (Usted trabaja en un supermercado moderno.)
(Pagan bien.)

E Profesiones

¿Qué profesión? Complete y traduzca al inglés.
What profession? Fill in the letters and translate into English.

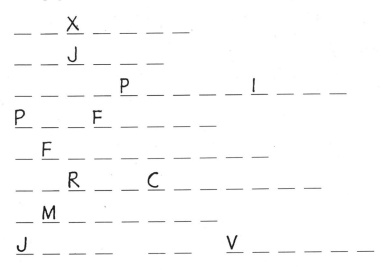

_ _ X _ _ _ _

_ _ J _ _ _

_ _ _ _ P _ _ _ _ _ I _ _ _

P _ _ F _ _ _ _ _

_ F _ _ _ _ _ _ _ _

_ _ R _ _ C _ _ _ _ _ _

_ M _ _ _ _ _

J _ _ _   _ _   V _ _ _ _ _

F Libro de textos, p. 22

G Numbers 20–99 · ¶ 14

- Trace and then join up the dots in the following order:

veinte – treinta y cinco – veintinueve – setenta – sesenta – sesenta y siete – cincuenta y dos – setenta y seis – noventa – cincuenta y tres – noventa y nueve – treinta y ocho – sesenta y cinco – cuarenta y uno – cincuenta – veintitrés – setenta y dos – sesenta y ocho – veinte

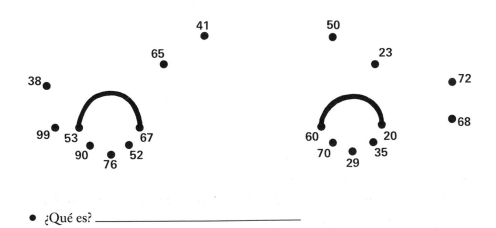

- ¿Qué es? _____

11 . . . van al cine

A Libro de textos, p. 23 ('Conteste a las preguntas.')

B ¿Qué hora es? · ¶ 15

If you wish to learn more about telling the time, see
¶ 15.

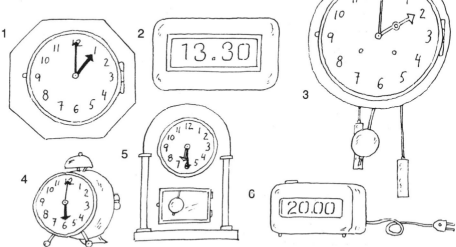

Some common first names and how they are used in ordinary speech:

Mercedes	Merche	Concepción	Concha
Josefa	Pepa	Encarnación	Encarna
Dolores	Lola	José	Pepe
Pilar	Pili	Francisco	Paco
Ana María	Ana Mari	Rafael	Rafa
Trinidad	Trini	Javier	Javi

C Ir a · ¶ 54, ¶ 1 D

1 Traduzca al español. (Use: *vosotros*)

– Where are you going?
○ To <u>the bank</u>.
– Are you going by bus?
○ No, we're going on foot.

2 After correction, practise the dialogue. Then for *the bank* substitute:

- the cinema
- the chemist's
- the supermarket
- the station

Now practise with the *ustedes* form.
Use different words for forms of transport (see exercise 5 B on page 13).

Cines

Sesión numerada

GRAN VÍA. Gran Vía, 66 (Centro)
Metro Santo Domingo/Tel. 247 10 29
2.30, 6 y 9.30
Un perro andaluz.
Una película clásica de Luis Buñuel.
Mayores de 16 años.

LOPE DE VEGA. Gran Vía, 55 (Centro) Metro Santo Domingo/Tel.
247 20 11
4,30, 7 y 10.
El estanque dorado con Henry Fonda,
K. Hepburn y Jane Fonda.
Tolerada.

V.O. Subtituladas

BENAVENTE. Climatizado. Plaza
Vázquez Mella, 3/Parking Infantas,
detrás Hortaleza, 24/Metro Gran Vía/
Tel. 228 28 64
8.30 y 10.30
Persona. Una película del director
sueco Ingmar Bergman.
Mayores de 18 años.

PEQUEÑO CINESTUDIO. Magallanes, 1 Metro Quevedo. Tel. 447 29 20
4, 6, 8 y 10.00
Lola. De Rainer Fassbinder, Alemania.
Mayores de 18 años.

Sesión continua

APOLO. Fernández de los Ríos, 34
(Chamberi)
Metro Quevedo/Tel. 447 68 18
4.30, 6.30, 8.30 y 10.30
*Las eróticas aventuras de Robinson
Crusoe.*
"S" Una película divertida.

CRISTAL. Bravo Murillo, 120
4, 6, 8 y 10
Las largas vacaciones del 36 de
Jaime Camino.
Una película sobre la guerra civil.
Tolerada.

VOCABULARIO

sesión numerada – *separate performance,
   with seats booked*
sesión continua – *continuous performance*
V.O. (= versión original) subtitulada
   – *original version with subtitles*
películas 'S' – *sex films*

24

D ¿Al cine?

1 Escriban el diálogo y representen la escena.

A	B
Suggest that you go to the cinema.	
	Say that you don't know. Ask what's on.
Say *a film by Buñuel*.	
	Say 'Oh yes.' Ask what it's called.
Say what it's called.	
	Repeat the title. Ask which cinema.
Say the name of the cinema.	
	Ask where it is.
Give the address.	
	Say that you'll go. (*Sí, vamos.*)

2 Make up several dialogues, substituting *a film by Buñuel* by:

- a film about the Civil War
- a film with Jane Fonda and her father, Henry Fonda, in it
- a film from Germany
- a film by Ingmar Bergman, the Swedish producer
- an entertaining film

E Adivinanza

Tres latinoamericanos están en el aeropuerto de Caracas. Una mujer pregunta: ¿Adónde van ustedes? Los tres contestan la misma cosa pero el mexicano va a México, el argentino va a Argentina y el chileno va a Chile.
¿Qué contestan los tres hombres?
(Solución página 119.)

VOCABULARIO

adivinanza (f) *riddle*
la misma cosa *the same thing*
solución (f) *solution*

12 En el Paseo del Prado

A   Libro de textos, p. 24 ('Compre …')

B   Numbers 100–500 · ¶ 14

Lea:

1 100	6 100 libros	11 437 revistas
2 200	7 100 pesetas	12 500 habitantes
3 350	8 150 pesetas	13 500 pesetas
4 475	9 210 coches	
5 500	10 320 periódicos	

C   En el quiosco

Compre usted un tebeo. Trabajen de dos en dos.
Buy a comic.

TBO
Super Mortadelo
Spider-Man
Jaimito
Pato Donald

(cont.)

A	B
Choose a comic.	
	Say that the comic A has chosen isn't available. Say you're sorry. Say which ones you do have.
Ask for one or several of those B suggests.	
	Say what they cost. Say something appropriate when you hand over the comic(s).
Say thank you. Hand over 500 pesetas.	
	Count out the change as you hand it back.

D Libro de textos, p. 25 ('A ver si ...')

E Verbos y pronombres · ¶ 34 A (*-ar* verbs), ¶ 63 (*tener*), ¶ 54 (*ir*), ¶ 18 (personal pronouns)

Rellene con todas las formas de los verbos **trabajar, tener, ir** y de los pronombres personales. *Fill in the missing forms of* **trabajar, tenir, ir** *and the personal pronouns.*

			tener	*ir*
infinitive		_____	*tener*	*ir* _____
singular 1	_____	_____	_____	_____
2	_____	*trabajas*	_____	_____
	él _____			
3	_____	_____	_____	_____
	usted _____			
plural 1	*nosotros,-as* _____		*tenemos* _____	_____
2	*vosotros,-as* _____		_____	*vais* _____
	ellos _____			
3	*ellas* _____	_____	*tienen* _____	_____
	ustedes _____			

F Verbos en *-ar* · ¶ 34 A, F

Write down ten verbs conjugated like *trabajar*.
Then write a sentence using each verb.

In most Spanish-American countries, *ustedes* is also used as a form of address to several people to each of whom you say *tú*.
So this is what Spanish school books published in, for instance, the USA, often look like:

THE PRESENT OF hablar AND estudiar

	hablar			estudiar	
(Yo)	hablo	inglés.	(Yo)	estudio	inglés.
(Tú)	hablas	inglés.	(Tú)	estudias	inglés.
(Usted) (El) (Ella)	habla	inglés.	(Usted) (El) (Ella)	estudia	inglés.
(Nosotros) (Nosotras)	hablamos	inglés.	(Nosotros) (Nosotras)	estudiamos	inglés.
(Ustedes) (Ellos) (Ellas)	hablan	inglés.	(Ustedes) (Ellos) (Ellas)	estudian	inglés.

Nota: *vosotros.* In Spain, *vosotros* is used to address two or more people with whom one uses *tú*.

 G Entrevistas

1   The use of *tú* is becoming increasingly widespread, although *usted* is still used out of respect or politeness in formal situations.

2   Practise asking questions of someone to whom you cannot say *tú* in Spanish. Work in pairs. One interviews, the other replies. Exchange rôles after interview 1.
A's instructions are written below. B's instructions are on page 119.

You are A:

Interview 1
Ask B...

- what her name is
- from which town she comes
- where she works
- if she speaks English
- how much she earns
- how many hours a week she works
- if she goes to work by car

Interview 2
Answer B's questions.

You are called Pedro González
- are from Barcelona
- are a teacher of English
- speak Castilian, English and Catalan
- have 18 lessons a week
- earn 60,000 pesetas a month
- go by bus – but walk from the bus-stop to work

Practise until the interviews run smoothly!

3   Now try to make up your own interviews. Use an imaginary person or someone you know.

13 Los meses del año

After p. 26

A La fecha · ¶ 16 A

Lea las fechas como en el ejemplo. *Read out the dates as in the example.*

– ¿Qué fecha es hoy?

○ Hoy es <u>el veintiséis de octubre</u>.

1 26.10	6 17.7	11 28.2
2 1.9	7 1.1	12 23.6
3 15.5	8 21.8	13 11.11
4 6.1	9 12.10	14 25.12
5 3.4	10 30.3	

B Los meses

Construya diálogos como en el ejemplo.

– A ver si adivinas cuándo es mi santo.

○ No sé. ¿En <u>febrero</u>?

– Más tarde.

○ ¿En <u>abril</u>?

– Antes.

– ¿En <u>marzo</u>?

– Eso es, en marzo.

1 febrero – abril – marzo
2 junio – agosto – julio
3 octubre – diciembre – noviembre
4 diciembre – febrero – enero
5 marzo – mayo – abril

> In Spanish-speaking countries, people celebrate their saint's day more than their birthday. The days of the year carry the names of different Catholic saints.

C Crucigrama

¿Cómo se dice "Many happy returns of the day" en español? Rellene con los nombres de nueve meses.

How do you say 'Many happy returns of the day' in Spanish? Fill in the names of nine of the months of the year.

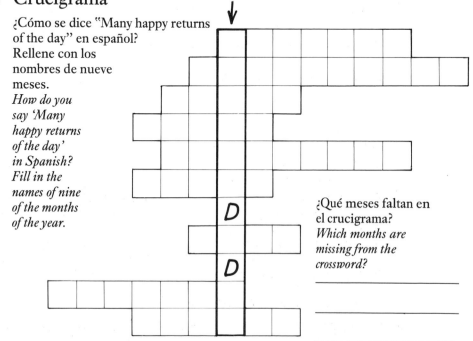

¿Qué meses faltan en el crucigrama? *Which months are missing from the crossword?*

Primer día de clase

D Ser · ¶ 62

Rellene con las formas del verbo *ser*.

(Teléfono: rrrrrrr)

Soledad	¿Sí?
Ana	Hola, ¹_____ Ana. ¿²_____ tú, Soledad?
S	Sí, ³_____ yo. Hola chica. ¿Qué hay?
A	Oye, ¿vamos todos a la playa?
S	¿Por qué no? Vamos en mi coche. ¿Cuántos ⁴_____ vosotros?
A	⁵_____ cinco. Jaime, Luis, Eva, Trini y yo.
S	¿Jaime y Luis?
A	⁶_____ mis primos. ⁷_____ muy simpáticos.
S	Bueno, vamos pues.

E Pronunciación *j, g* · ¶ 83

Lea:

Juan José Gimeno,
un joven ingeniero argentino,
y su mujer Julia
trabajan juntos en Gibraltar
en junio y julio.

(ingeniero – *engineer*)

14 El centro de España

A Central Spain

Say what you know about Central Spain, in English.

B Make pairs

Match each word in the left-hand column with one in the right.

1	acueducto	a	Toledo
2	molinos de viento	b	la Meseta
3	El Greco	c	La Mancha
4	cultivos de trigo	d	Valladolid
5	el 40% del territorio español	e	la provincia de Cuenca
6	un embalse	f	Navacerrada
7	pistas y telesquís	g	Segovia
8	FASA-Renault	h	La Mancha

The Romans

In 218 B.C., Roman soldiers attacked the Mediterranean coast of the Iberian peninsula in order to push back Hannibal's troops. The latter had earlier tried to take Rome by marching up through the Iberian peninsula, crossing first the Pyrenees, then the Alps. For 200 years, the Romans continued to conquer more and more of the peninsula. From the birth of Christ and for 400 years to come, it was ruled by the Romans. They founded towns and built roads, bridges and aqueducts. They also gave Spain her name (Latin: *Hispania*), her language and the Christian faith.

15 Salamanca

After p. 32

A   Libro de textos, p. 33 ('Describa el dibujo.')

B Possession · ¶6

- Traduzca al inglés:
1 los padres de Merche
2 el coche del director
3 el dueño de la librería
4 la casa de los Gómez
5 la madre de las chicas

- Traduzca al español:
6   The capital of Spain
7   Mr Ibarra's passport
8   The boys' teacher
9   The key of the room
10 The director of the bank

- What does *de* express?

C Entre tú y yo 1 (Expressions of place)

Trabajen de dos en dos.

A describes the picture on page 119. Use the Spanish expressions for *behind, in front of, between, in, on the right, on the left.* **B** listens and fills in a tracing of picture 1 on the right (page 33).

Then exchange rôles. **B** describes the picture on page 120. **A** listens and fills in a tracing of picture 2 on the right (page 33).

En Correos

D ¿Qué hora es? · ¶ 15

Lea:

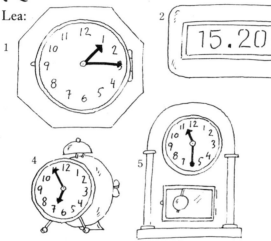

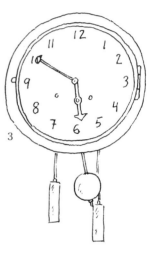

E La hora

Mire el mapa. En Barcelona son las doce.
¿Qué hora es. . .?
1 ¿en Santiago de Chile?   **2** ¿en Buenos Aires?   **3** ¿en San Francisco?

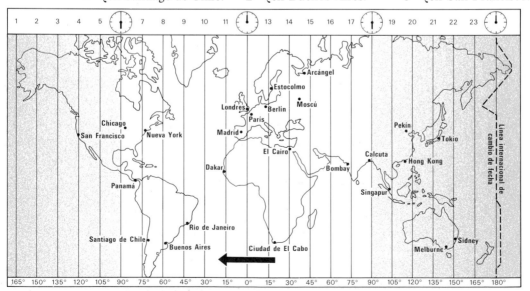

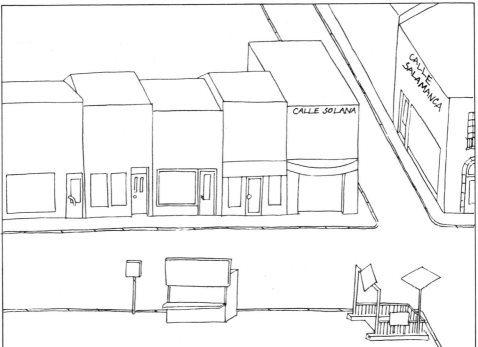

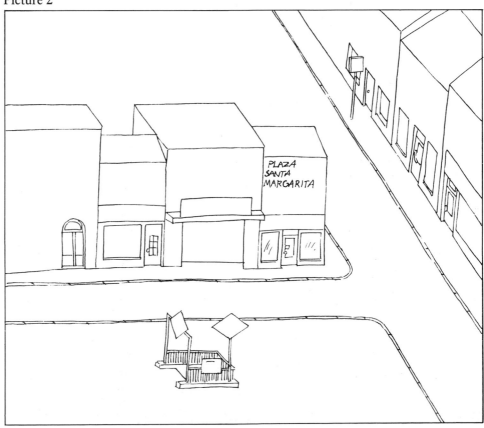

16 Librería Papelería

A Libro de textos, p. 35 ('Conteste a las preguntas.')

B Adjectives · ¶ 8–9

1 Traduzca al español (masc. sing.):

slim	white
tall	interesting
big	red
huge	expensive
small	cheap
old	good
new	famous
black	splendid

2 Construya frases como en los ejemplos:

El chico es *alto*. Los coches son *viejos*.

Pedro ...	La catedral ...
Los chicos ...	La farmacia ...
María ...	La maleta ...
Las hermanas ...	Los libros ...
La ciudad ...	El turismo ...

C Numbers · ¶ 14

Lea:

140 pesetas	777 postales
500 pesetas	818 bolígrafos
550 libros	990 carpetas
660 sobres	1.000 pesetas

D ¿Cuánto cuesta? · ¶ 14 (numbers), ¶ 8–9 (adjectives), ¶ 4 (otro)

Compre usted en la librería. Trabajen de dos en dos.

– ¿Cuánto cuesta el plano?
○ 350 pesetas.
– Es muy caro. ¿No tiene otro?
○ Sí, el plano que está allí.
  Es bueno y barato, 150 pesetas.
– Muy bien.
○ ¿Algo más?
– No, gracias. Está bien.

Cambie	*el plano*	*350*	*150*
por	la carpeta	210	170
	los bolígrafos	45	21
	los lápices	33	16

E Escuche.

¿Qué compra el señor? Complete el texto.

– ¿Y usted, señor? ¿Qué desea?

○ ¿ ^{1}_____ usted el último ^{2}_____ de Vargas Llosa?

– Sí, sí, aquí está.

○ ¿ ^{3}_____ cuesta?

– A ver … ^{4}_____ pesetas.

○ Muy bien.

– ^{5}_____ más?

○ ^{6}_____ ^{7}_____ sobres, por favor.

– ¿^{8}_____ ?

○ Sí.

– Tenga. ^{9}_____ pesetas.

○ Ah, perdone, ¿no tiene una ^{10}_____ de la Casa de las Conchas?

– ¿^{11}_____ una? ^{12}_____ . Son ^{13}_____ pesetas en total.

○ Muchas gracias.

– A usted.

35

17 Desayuno en la cafetería

A   Libro de textos, p. 37 ('¿Qué desea . . .?')

B   Libro de textos, p. 37 ('¿Qué desayunan . . .?')

After line 21

C ¿Muy o mucho? · ¶ 13

● Traduzca al inglés:
1   El actor es muy famoso y trabaja mucho.
2   Muy bien, muchas gracias.
3   Tiene mucho trabajo; bebe mucho café pero fuma mucho más.

● When, in Spanish, do we use *muy* and when *mucho*?
Give the rule.

● Traduzca al español:
4   The ballpoint pen is very cheap.
5   It does not cost very much.
6   But the pencil is very much cheaper.
7   Pilar works very hard.
8   She studies a lot of English.
9   She already speaks English very well.

D ¿Qué desayuna usted?

Tell a friend what you have for breakfast. Then ask him/her what he/she has for breakfast.

VOCABULARIO
yoghurt   yogur (m)
egg   huevo
margarine   margarina
butter   mantequilla
jam or marmalade   mermelada
a slice of toast   una tostada
bread   pan
cereals   Corn Flakes (*or other brands*)

E Pronunciación · ¶ 86 (entonación/intonation)

1   Look up ¶ 86. Listen to the tape and repeat.
2   Read lines 7–21 of the dialogue again. Pay special attention to intonation.

18 Un día completo

A   Libro de textos, p. 38 ('Conteste a las preguntas.')

B   Libro de textos, p. 38 ('Angel habla de sí mismo.')

C   ¿A qué hora? · ¶ 15

Pregunte y conteste como en el ejemplo.

– ¿A qué hora cierra <u>el banco</u>?
○ <u>A las dos.</u>

el banco	14.00	la farmacia	20.30
el súper	20.00	el bar	22.30
la oficina	17.45	el restaurante	24.00
la cafetería	23.30		

D   Revision of verbs

Complete con la forma correcta de los verbos al margen.
Fill in the correct form of the verbs in the margin.

Cristina [1]_____ en el supermercado   *go in (= enter)*

para [2]_____ con su amiga Teresa.   *talk*
C   Hola, Teresa. ¿Cómo estás?

T   Regular. [3]_____ mucho trabajo.   *I have*

C   ¿A qué hora [4]_____ hoy?   *do you finish*
T   A las 20.30.
C   ¡A las 20.30! ¿No [5]_____ a las 20.00?   *do you close*

T   El súper [6]_____ a las 20.00, pero   *close*

nosotros [7]_____ hasta las 20.30.   *work*

¿Por qué [8]_____?   *do you ask*

C   [9]_____ una película americana en   *they are showing (= giving)*

el Lux. ¿[10]_____?   *shall we go*

T   No [11]_____. ¿A qué hora [12]_____?   *I know; it begins*
C   A las 21.30.

T   [13]_____ yo también. Pero antes [14]_____   *I'm coming (= going); I have to*
pasar por casa.
C   Estupendo.

E ¿Acento o no? · ¶ 84–85

Re-write this short text, putting accents where necessary. (Accents are not always necessary on capital letters.) Then make a rule for stress in Spanish.

LAURA GUZMAN TIENE MUCHO QUE HACER HOY. SU AMIGA MARIA ESTA EN EL HOSPITAL. POR LA TARDE LAURA VA AL HOSPITAL, PERO ANTES VA A UNA LIBRERIA PARA COMPRAR UN LIBRO EN INGLES. COMPRA ADEMAS UNAS POSTALES. DESPUES ENTRA EN UNA CAFETERIA PARA TOMAR UN CAFE. VA EN BICICLETA AL HOSPITAL. MARIA ESTA EN LA HABITACION NUMERO 8. CUANDO LLEGA LAURA, EL MEDICO ESTA ALLI.

Now write questions in Spanish to a friend. Ask:
1 where Laura's friend is.
2 what her friend's name is.
3 when Laura is going to the hospital.
4 what Laura is going to buy.
5 why she goes into a café afterwards.
6 how she is going to get to the hospital.
7 which room her friend is in.
8 who is there when Laura arrives.

F Escuche.

Una canción. *A song.*

Escuche la cinta y rellene.

De esta manera lavamos ¹_____
así, así, así, así,
de esta manera lavamos ²_____

el ³_____ por la ⁴_____.

De esta manera planchamos ⁵_____
ayudo así, así, así,
de esta manera planchamos ⁶_____

el ⁷_____ por la ⁸_____.

De esta manera cosemos ⁹_____
así, así, así, así,
de esta manera cosemos ¹⁰_____

el ¹¹_____ por la ¹²_____.

De esta manera hacemos ¹³_____

ayudo a mi ¹⁴_____ así, así,

de esta manera hacemos ¹⁵_____

el ¹⁶_____.

de esta manera
in this way
lavar *to wash*
así *like this*

planchar *to iron*
ayudar *to help*

coser *to sew*

38

De esta manera ¹⁷_____ las compras,

ayudo a mi ¹⁸_____ así, así,

de esta manera ¹⁹_____ las compras,

el ²⁰_____.

las compras *shopping*

De esta manera limpiamos ²¹_____
ayudo así, así, así,
de esta manera limpiamos ²²_____

el ²³_____.

limpiar *to clean*

De esta manera nos ²⁴_____ a misa,
así, así, así, así,
de esta manera nos ²⁵_____ a misa,

el ²⁶_____.

la misa *mass*

19 Una cita

A Libro de textos, p. 39

After line 8

B Estar · ¶ 33 C, ¶ 51

- Traduzca al inglés:

  ¿Cómo está usted?
  Clara y su padre no están todavía.
  Lima está en Perú.

- What are the different meanings of *estar*? In what way are the forms different from a regular *-ar* verb?
- Traduzca al español:

Luisa has lunch at the Estrella bar. Juan and José come in. They are friends of Paco, her brother.

Luisa: Hi, how are you?
J & J: Fine. How are you?
Luisa: Fine, thanks.
Juan: Is Paco here in Barcelona now?
Luisa: No, he's in Ubrique.
José: And where's Ubrique?
Luisa: In Andalusia.

C ¿A qué hora?

Say in Spanish when

1 the Spanish
2 the English

have breakfast, lunch and dinner.

> ## Vía Véneto
>
> *COMIDAS*
>
> *Desayuno 8h — 10h30*
> *Almuerzo 13h — 15h*
> *Cena 20h — 22h*
>
> *RESTAURANTE * TERRAZA * BAR*

D Libro de textos, p. 39 (Using the above information . . .')

E Palabras y frases 1

Words and phrases

When you wish to express yourself fluently in the spoken language, it is useful to know some special words and phrases. Sometimes the same expressions do not exist in Spanish and English. Sometimes there is no exact equivalent at all in the other language. You have already come across some of these words and phrases. Try to find what you say when you . . .

1 need a moment to think
2 want to attract the attention of
  a someone you say *tú* to
  b someone you say *usted* to
3 don't know, hesitate
4 are sorry about something
5 realize something is right
6 ask a favour
7 need support
8 think something is good
9 think something is awfully good
10 agree
11 protest
12 express surprise
13 reply to thanks
14 explain

no sé

es que . . .

por favor

bueno ¿ verdad ?

ah sí, claro

no, hombre, no   *pues*   *vaya*

estupendo   *no, mujer*

¿ no ?   *oye* *mire* *de nada*

lo siento *eso sí*

eso es *a ver* *muy bien*

F Llamada telefónica

Invent a telephone conversation. Try to use words and phrases from Exercise E. Use *tú*.

A	B
Dial a number, saying six numbers.	
	Reply.
Greet B. Say who you are. Ask if Vicente is at home.	
	Say it is you.
Say 'Oh, it's you, is it?' Ask how Vicente is.	
	Say you are well. Ask how A is.
Say you are very well. Ask if you (*pl*) are going to the cinema tomorrow.	
	Say you're sorry, but your English course starts tomorrow. Suggest going today.
Say that's fine. Suggest that you go to the Cinestudio.	
	Ask what film is on.
Say it's a very good American film. Suggest that you go at eight o'clock.	
	Say no, you have dinner at eight o'clock. Suggest you go to the ten o'clock performance.
Say that's fine. 'Quarter to ten, then.'	
	Ask where.
Say at the entrance.	
	Say goodbye.

20 El este de España

Conteste a las preguntas.

Lines 1–5

1 ¿Qué lenguas se hablan en el este de España?

Lines 6–28 (País Valenciano)

2 En el País Valenciano, ¿qué trabajo tiene una gran parte de la población?
3 ¿Cómo es la tierra?
4 ¿Llueve mucho?
5 ¿Qué fruta se cultiva en las huertas?
6 ¿Adónde se exporta?
7 Además de fruta, ¿qué produce la tierra de Valencia?
8 ¿Qué ingredientes hay en la paella valenciana?

Lines 29–39 (Cataluña)

9 Aquí hay tres mapas que muestran la relación que existe entre Cataluña y el resto de España. ¿Qué palabras corresponden a las tres cifras de porcentaje?

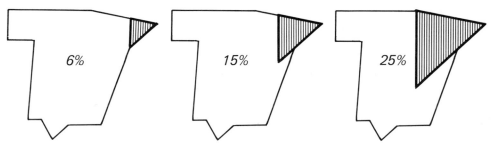

Here are three maps showing the relationship between Catalonia and the rest of Spain. Which words correspond to the three percentages?

10 En Cataluña, ¿qué trabajo tiene una gran parte de la población?
11 Muchos son inmigrantes. ¿De dónde son?

Picture captions, p. 42

12 ¿Cómo se llama la capital de Cataluña?
13 ¿Cuántos habitantes tiene?
14 ¿Cómo se llama la calle más popular de Barcelona?
15 ¿Qué venden allí?
16 La Sagrada Familia, ¿de quién es la obra?
17 ¿Dónde está?

Lines 40–46 (Islas Baleares)

18 ¿Cómo se llaman las cuatro Islas Baleares?
19 ¿Por qué van muchos turistas allí?

21 De paso por Elche

After line 12

A Verbos en *-er* · ¶ 34 B, F

Complete las frases.

1 Los turistas _____.   *are thirsty*

2 _____ algo.   *They want to drink*

3 El guía dice que _____ descansar   *they can*

un rato y _____ o   *eat*

_____ algo en el bar.   *drink*

4 El niño _____.   *is hungry*

5 El guía _____ que también   *thinks*
hay bocadillos en el bar.

After p. 44

B Algo/no ... nada · ¶ 29 A

Hagan ustedes un diálogo entre el cliente y el camarero.
Make up a dialogue between the customer and the waiter.
Miren la lista de precios de la página 36 del libro de textos.

El cliente	El camarero
Call for the waiter.	
	Say something which shows you can take the order.
Order what you want to drink.	
	Ask if the customer wants anything else.
Say that you're hungry and would like something to eat.	
	Suggest a sandwich.
Order the sandwich you want.	
	Ask if the customer wants anything else.
Say you don't want anything else; it's fine as it is.	
	Say 'right away'.

C Libro de textos, p. 45 ('Cuente ...')

D Crucigrama

Rellene el crucigrama y el diálogo. *Fill in the crossword and the dialogue.*

– Tengo ¹........................... . Quiero comer.
○ Yo ²........................ . ³........................ hacer unos
⁴...................... .
¿⁵.................... algo en casa?
– ⁶.................... hay pan y ⁷.................... .
○ El queso no me ⁸.................... mucho. ¿No hay ⁹....................?
– A ver . . . Sí, pero no hay mucho.
○ Entonces yo como un bocadillo de jamón y tú ¹⁰.................... de queso.
– ¿Qué bebemos? ¿Té?
○ ¹¹.................... leche.
– ¹²¡....................!, no hay.
○ Bueno, entonces, un té.

E Pronunciación *b, v* · ¶ 83

Lea:

En Bogotá, en Colombia,
venden bolígrafos
buenos y bastante
baratos.

Bárbara ÿ su abuela
trabajan en Barcelona,
en un banco.
En febrero
van a Valladolid,
en avión,
y en abril
van a Valencia,
en barco.

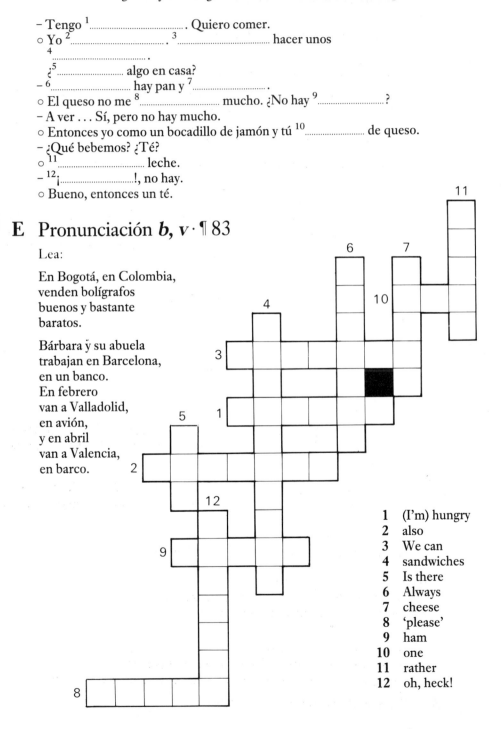

1   (I'm) hungry
2   also
3   We can
4   sandwiches
5   Is there
6   Always
7   cheese
8   'please'
9   ham
10 one
11 rather
12 oh, heck!

22 Llamada telefónica

A Libro de textos, p. 46

B Libro de textos, p. 46 ('Llame por teléfono y reserve . . .')

C Libro de textos, p. 47 ('Usted está en España . . .')

D Una llamada de un minuto

Usted va a llamar a una persona en España. Tiene algo muy importante que decir, pero tiene dinero sólo para un minuto.
You have to telephone someone in Spain. You have something very important to say, but you only have enough money for one minute.

Make up what you want to say, or use the following as aids:

- your name is . . .
- you're telephoning from . . .
- you are a friend of the person's son/daughter who is studying in England.
- you want to say that the son/daughter is coming to Barajas that evening at . . . They will take the bus to the terminal and will wait there. They have a lot of luggage.

How far did you get in a minute?
How long does it take you to give the full message?

E Conversación por teléfono

Trabajen de dos en dos.

A:
Usted está en un hotel de Valencia. (Mire la guía de hoteles de la página 46 del libro de textos.) Usted tiene que llamar a un amigo español/una amiga española en Castellón de la Plana.

(Practise before telephoning. Choose a hotel. Remember to check whether your friend has the right address, telephone number and time when you are to meet.)

1 Ring up.
2 Say who you are. Ask to speak to your friend.
3 Ask how he/she is.
4 Say which hotel you're in.
5 Ask if your friend can be there tomorrow at . . .
6 Say the address and telephone number.

B:
You answer the telephone.
You answer in the affirmative to your friend's questions.
Jot down the address etc if you like, to make sure you have it correct.

Then exchange rôles.

España   Argentina   México   Otros muchos países

En todos los países no dicen lo mismo.   (lo mismo—*the same*)

F Interrogative words · ¶ 32

Muchos niños preguntan mucho.
Usted aparca delante de una gasolinera.
Mientras espera llega un niño. Pregunta y pregunta . . .
¿Qué pregunta para tener estas respuestas?
What does he ask, to get the following answers? (Use **tú**.)

	El niño	*Tú*
1	....	/Soy/de Alicante.
2	....	/Me llamo/Alfonso Montalbán.
3	....	/Vivo/en las afueras de Alicante.
4	....	/El coche/es de mi hermano.
5	....	/Voy/a Castellón.
6	....	Porque hay una fiesta allí.
7	....	Mañana.

G Requests · ¶ 45 A–B

- You have met various requests in the exercises and texts. What do the following mean?

conteste   rellene   escuche
pregunte   reserve   compre

What are the corresponding infinitives?

In Spanish, the present subjunctive is used as a request with *usted*. You will be learning about this in **¡Ya! 2**. At present it is sufficient that you understand what the requests mean. As you have seen, the *ar* verbs in the present subjunctive end in *-e*. *Er* and *ir* verbs end in *-a*.

- What do the following mean?

describa   tenga   traduzca
escriba   oiga   introduzca
déme   diga

Sometimes the spelling changes. See ¶ 89.

- What do the following mean?

descuelgue   marque

What are the infinitives of *descuelgue* and *marque*?

23 El tiempo . . . y las estaciones del año

A Dos calendarios

Rellene con el nombre de los meses y de las estaciones.

1 Europa

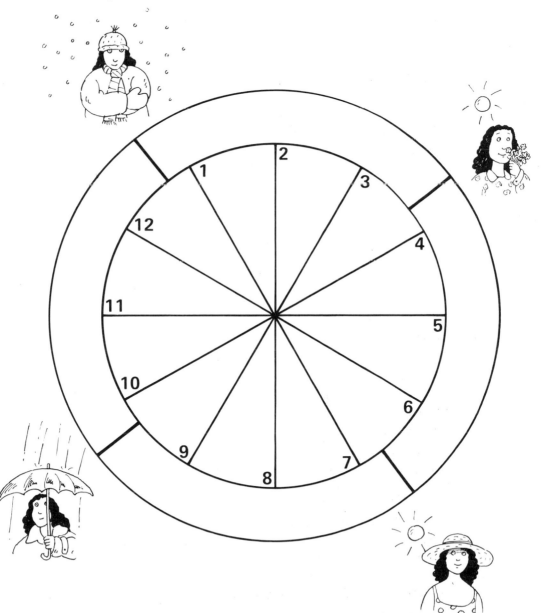

2 Chile, Argentina
Make up a similar calendar for the southern hemisphere.

B ¿Qué tiempo hace? · ¶ 68 B

C Bueno · ¶ 9 C

Pregunte y conteste como en el ejemplo.

– <u>El hotel Miramar</u> es un buen hotel, ¿no?
○ Sí, es muy bueno.

El hotel Miramar

La pensión La Valenciana
El hostal California
El restaurante El Rincón

24 En la playa

After dialogue 1

A Languages, members of the family · ¶ 3 J

If you travel abroad, you are often asked whether you and your companion can speak the language of the country. So practise this dialogue, substituting other languages and other people.

– ¿Habla usted <u>español</u>, señorita?
○ Sí, un poco. Estudio español en Londres.
– ¿Y su <u>novio</u> también?
○ Él no. Pero entiende un poco.

español	*novio*	
inglés	hermana	padre
catalán	amigo	madre
alemán	primo	hermano
francés	mujer	primos
	novia	

After dialogue 2

B Countries · ¶ 2 B; Nationalities · ¶ 8

● Conteste a las preguntas.

1	¿De qué país es la señora Brown? (*De . . .*)	¿De qué nacionalidad es entonces? (*Es . . .*)
2	¿el Sr. Brandt?	
3	¿la Sra. Svensson?	
4	¿la Srta. Sánchez?	
5	¿la Srta. Atze?	
6	¿De qué país son los señores Dupont?	¿De qué nacionalidad son?

● Complete las frases.

7   El señor Platinga es holandés. Es de ....
8   El señor Hederup es danés. Es de ....
9   La señora Sorstad es noruega. Es de ....
10 El señor Koponen es finlandés. Es de ....
11 La señorita Soares es portuguesa. Es de ....
12 El señor Moretti es italiano. Es de ....

● Escriba los nombres de los países en el mapa.
(Look at the map on page 5 of
the Students' Book.)

la Sra. Svensson

la Sra. Brown

la Srta. Atze

el Sr. Brandt

los Sres. Dupont

la Srta. Sánchez

C Languages · ¶ 3 J; Nationalities · ¶ 8

En la playa venden periódicos. ¿Qué periódicos venden?
Complete el diálogo.

– ¿Tiene periódicos en [1]......................?   *German*

o No, lo siento. No quedan. ¿Es usted

[2]......................?   *German*

– No, soy suizo.

o ¿No habla [3]......................? Tenemos Le Monde.   *French*

– No, entonces mejor un periódico [4]...................... .   *Spanish*

   Déme el Avui.

o Pero si el Avui está en [5]...................... .   *Catalan*

   Tenga El País, que está en [6]...................... .   *Castilian*

(avui *catalán* = hoy)

After dialogue 4

D Verbos en *-ir* · ¶ 34 C, F

Which forms of *subir, escribir, vivir* are correct in the following sentences?

1 Mamá y yo .... una postal a Pedro.
2 Los dos españoles .... ahora en Francia.
3 Ana y tú .... a pie, ¿no?

What are the other forms in the present tense? Which forms are different from the *-er* verbs?

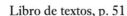 **E** Libro de textos, p. 51

F Cuente.

1 Do you like imagining things?
Write a few lines about one of these two people.
If you want to, use the questions below.

¿De qué nacionalidad es?
¿Dónde vive?
¿Cómo se llama?
¿Cuántos años tiene?
¿Tiene familia?
¿Dónde trabaja?
¿Qué profesión tiene?
¿El trabajo es interesante, aburrido, . . .?
¿Pagan bien, mal, . . .?
¿Dónde está ahora? (en el aeropuerto, en la aduana, en
la cocina, cerca de un quiosco, en un bar, en casa de . . .)
¿Adónde va?
¿Por qué?

2 Use a photograph of your own or a newspaper-cutting.
Ask a friend questions and let him/her imagine who the person is.

25 Dos postales . . .

After postcard 1

A Libro de textos, p. 52 ('¿Qué escriben Carlos y Elisa?')

B Years · ¶ 16 C

Lea los años.

1 1983 mil novecientos ochenta y tres
2 1967
3 1945
4 1571
5 1492
6 1936
7 1939

C Fechas · ¶ 16 A, D

Lea las fechas.

1 Santander, 3.2 1983
   Santander, tres de febrero
   de mil novecientos ochenta y tres
2 Madrid, 3.5 1808
3 San Salvador, 12.10 1492
4 Lepanto, 7.10 1571
5 Burgos, 30.7 1936
6 Madrid, 6.12 1978

After postcard 2

D Future · ¶ 38

• ¿Qué van a hacer el domingo? Pregunten y contesten como en el ejemplo.

Ask what the other people *are going to do*. Choose from the right-hand column.

– ¿Qué va a hacer <u>Pepe</u> el domingo?
○ Va a <u>ir al cine</u>.

Pepe	*ir al cine*
Pablo y Martín	alquilar un coche
tú y Felisa	regresar a la capital
la señorita Cavero	estudiar
	almorzar en casa de una amiga
	ir a la piscina
	trabajar extra

• Y usted, ¿qué va a hacer? ....

E Una postal

You are on holiday somewhere. Write and say:
• where you are
• what the weather is like
• how you are
• where you are staying (hotel, guest house, with . . . etc.)
• what you're going to do tomorrow
• how long you are staying

Remember to include the introductory and concluding phrases.

...y una carta de México

Before p. 53

F Reflexive verbs (1) · ¶ 26–27

Traduzca al español.

On the beach
- My name's Diego Peralta. What's yours?
○ My name's Soledad Parra.
- I'm staying here for a fortnight.
○ I've got to leave tomorrow.

Look up ¶ 26 and 27 and learn all the forms of the present tense.
Where is the reflexive pronoun placed with verbs in the present tense?
And where with the infinitive?

After the letter on p. 53

G Reflexive verbs (2) · ¶ 26–27

Rellene con la forma correcta de los verbos al margen.

Conversación en la discoteca

- ¿Cómo ^1_____?   *is your name*

○ ^2_____ María Isabel.   *My name is*

- ¿Y cómo ^3_____ tu hermana?   *is the name of*

○ ^4_____ Julia.   *Her name is*

- ^5_____ hasta la hora de cerrar?   *Are you staying*

○ No, ^6_____ sólo   *we're staying*
hasta las diez.

- ¿Por qué ^7_____ tan temprano?   *are you leaving*

○ Tenemos que ^8_____ a casa   *go*
porque papá y mamá

^9_____ mañana por la mañana.   *go away*
Van a México. Tenemos

que ^10_____ a las seis.   *get up*

H Una carta de México

Conteste a las preguntas (*letter on p. 53*).

1 ¿Quién escribe la carta?
2 ¿A quién escribe?

(cont.)

3 ¿Dónde está?
4 ¿Qué dice de esta ciudad?
5 ¿Qué estudia allí?
6 ¿Cuánto tiempo va a quedarse allí?
7 ¿Qué dice de su trabajo?
8 ¿Qué hace los fines de semana?
9 ¿Qué va a hacer este domingo?
10 ¿Qué más dice de su vida en México?

I Escuche.

¿Qué escribe Claudio a su amigo Bruno? Complete el texto.

México D.F., 10 de diciembre de 1983

¿ Sabes cuántos ^{1}.......................... tiene esta
^{2}.......................... ? ¡^{3}.......................... millones!
Pero esto no es nada. El año ^{4}..........................
va a ^{5}.......................... – dicen – ^{6}..........................
^{7}.......................... ^{8}.......... como toda España.
Bueno, ^{9}.......................... mucho y ¡^{10}..........................
una barbaridad.
Ah, ¡felices Navidades! Yo ^{11}..........................
las Navidades en Cancún. Espero ^{12}..........................
bañarme. Hoy ^{13}.......... allí ^{14}..........................
grados.
Chau   *Claudio*

Bruno Pereda
Avda. de Felipe II, 8
Madrid – 3

ESPAÑA

(bañarse – *to go swimming*; una barbaridad – *a terrific lot*)

	Turistas extranjeros que van a España	Turistas españoles que van al extranjero
1960	4.332363	2.149153
1970	21.267380	4.449881
1980	32.925110	17.705431

A Cuente.

Cuente usted lo que sabe de Andalucía con la ayuda de estas palabras:

Andalucía – región – produce – la tierra – latifundios – industria – emigran – centros turísticos – problemas – trabajo – árabes

B ¿Sí o no?

- If the following statements are true, you put SI, otherwise NO.
  For every reply you are given a letter of the alphabet.
  The letters form a word. What word?

Answer: _____

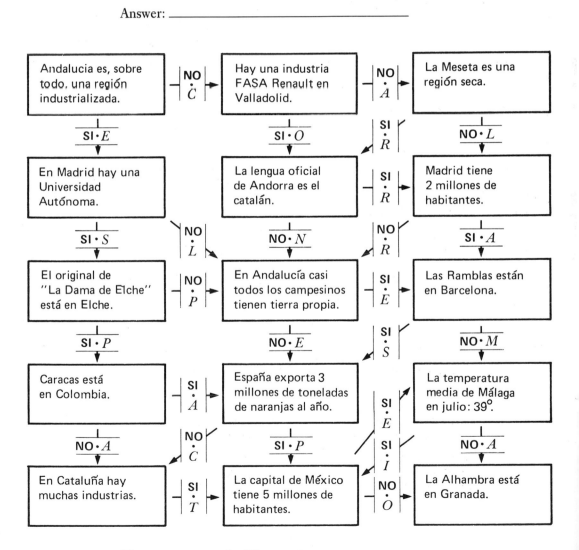

- If you can, correct the false statements.

27 Un campesino

After line 11

A   Libro de textos, p. 58 ('Juan Casares habla de sí mismo.')

After line 27

B   Libro de textos, p. 58 ('¿Qué va a hacer …?')

C   Libros de textos, p. 58 ('Describa el dibujo.')

D   Formation of words 1

It is easier to learn words if you think about which words belong to each other, for instance, llegar – *to arrive*, la llegada – *arrival*.

● Which nouns belong to the following verbs?
(Sometimes there are two.)

salir	cenar	desayunar
preguntar	comer	llamar
trabajar	almorzar	emigrar
ducharse	vivir	beber

● Which other nouns are related to these?

la caja	el farmacéutico	la hora
el libro	el turismo	

E La familia · ¶ 5 C

¿Quién es quién? Complete las frases.

1 "Me llamo Lola Guzmán. Tengo 11 años.
   Mi [1]............... se llama Esteban.
   Vicente Guzmán es mi [2]................ .
   Mis [3]............... se llaman Alfonso y Dolores.
   Pablo es mi [4]................ .
   Tengo cuatro [5]................ . Se llaman Pilar, Trini,
   Jaime y Pedro."

2 "Soy Vicente Guzmán.
   Mi [1]............... se llama Laura.
   Mi [2]............... Lola tiene 11 años y Esteban,
   mi [3]................ , tiene 13.
   Dolores y Alfonso son mis [4]................ .
   Tengo solamente una [5]................ , Mari Carmen.
   Ella tiene cuatro [6]................ .
   Mis [7]............... se llaman Pilar, Trini, Jaime y Pedro."

28 En la peluquería...

A Perfect tense -ar · ¶ 39 A; *tener que* · ¶ 63

Muchas personas han bajado al centro hoy.
¿Por qué?
Pregunte y conteste como en el ejemplo.

– Juan Casares, ¿por qué ha bajado hoy?
○ Porque tiene que ir al dentista.

Juan Casares	*ir al dentista*
los chicos	buscar trabajo
tú	ir al médico
tú y tu amigo	visitar a una tía
usted	alquilar un coche
los señores Martínez	ir al banco
tú	ir a la peluquería

Pili & Pepa
peluquería señora

lavar 2 00 ptas
marcar 550 ptas
peinar 2 50 ptas

marcar – *to set*
peinar – *to comb*

B Perfect tense -ar, -er, -ir · ¶ 39 A–C

Cuente lo que ha hecho Adolfo hoy.
Say what Adolfo has done today. Use the words below.

leer el periódico · almorzar en el bar de la playa · cenar con la familia · desayunar · regresar a las cinco · salir · tomar dos tazas de café · hablar por teléfono con su amigo Paco · ir al cine con Lola · ir a la playa

...y en casa de nuevo

C Libro de textos, p. 61 ('Cuente lo que ha hecho ...')

D *No ... nada* · ¶ 29 A; Perfect tense · ¶ 39

Pregunte y conteste como en el ejemplo.

– ¿Qué ha hecho <u>Pepe</u> hoy por la
  mañana?
○ Ha estudiado (trabajado).
– ¿Y por la tarde?
○ Por la tarde no ha hecho nada
  especial.

Pepe
tú
vosotros
el jefe
usted
los hijos
ustedes

E Cuente.

Cuente lo que ha hecho usted – hoy u otro día.
Say what you have done – today, or some other day.

F ¿Conoce usted a Leopoldo?

Complete el texto con el pretérito compuesto de los verbos al margen.
Fill in the perfect tense of the verbs in the margin.
Conteste después a la pregunta.

«Leopoldo se levanta siempre a las seis pero hoy

se ¹_____ media hora más tarde.   *levantar*
Ducharse le gusta mucho, un cuarto de hora

²_____ en la ducha.   *estar*

Cinco minutos más tarde ya se ³_____   *sentar*
a desayunar.

⁴_____ muy rápidamente, en cinco   *desayunar*
minutos.
La parada de autobuses está a dos minutos de su

puerta. ⁵_____ el número   *tomar*

quince que le ⁶_____ doce minutos   *dejar*
más tarde en el parque, exactamente donde empieza
el circuito de footing.
El footing le entusiasma a Leopoldo.

Hoy ⁷_____ cuatro vueltas en 18   *dar*
minutos.

(cont.)

¡Un récord personal! Después ⁸_____   *ir*
otra vez a la parada para volver a casa.

⁹_____ que esperar el autobús   *tener*
cinco minutos.»

● ¿Qué hora es cuando llega a casa? _____

VOCABULARIO

a dos minutos de   *two minutes away from*
el circuito de footing   *jogging circuit*
el footing le entusiasma   *he is very keen on jogging*

29 ¿Qué le pasa?

A El cuerpo humano

Fill in the names of the parts of the body you have already learnt.
If you like, you can also learn what the other parts are.

(el cuerpo humano – *the human body*)

la frente   los ojos
                la nariz
la garganta   la boca   el dedo
la espalda

B Doler · ¶ 74

Fill in the speech bubbles.

61

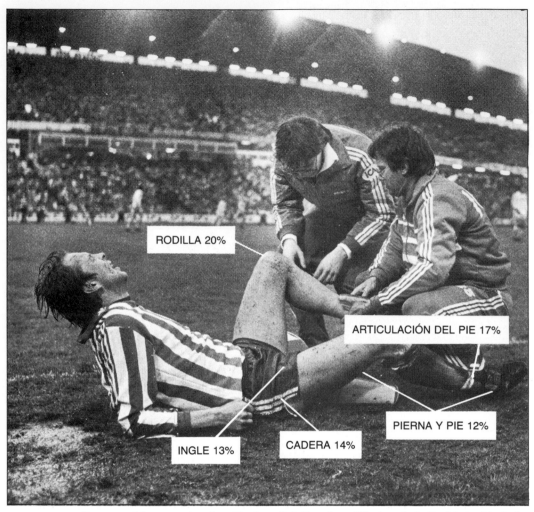

RODILLA 20%

ARTICULACIÓN DEL PIE 17%

PIERNA Y PIE 12%

INGLE 13%

CADERA 14%

Las partes del cuerpo más vulnerables de un futbolista: La rodilla, la articulación del pie, el ingle, la cadera y la pierna. (ingle – *groin*; cadera – *hip*)

C Le gusta. Le duele. Le pasa. · ¶ 74

- Some common verbs use different constructions in Spanish. What do the following three sentences mean?

1 El libro no le gusta.
2 Le duelen los ojos.
3 ¿Qué le pasa?

Literal translations would be:
The book does not to him please.   To him ache the eyes.   What to him is happening?

- Traduzca al español:
4 I've got a headache.
5 Her eyes ache.
6 Do your feet ache?
7 He doesn't like coffee.
8 She likes children.
9 What's wrong with you?

D El primer resfriado

Do you feel like this when you have a cold?
Translate the poem into English, using a dictionary.

Me duelen los ojos.
me duele el cabello,
me duele la punta
tonta de los dedos.

Y aquí en la garganta
una hormiga corre
con cien patas largas.
Ay, mi resfriado,
chaquetas, bufandas,
leche calentita
y doce pañuelos
y catorce mantas
y estarse muy quieto
junto a la ventana.

Me duelen los ojos,
me duele la espalda,
me duele el cabello,
me duele la tonta
punta de los dedos.

Celia Viñas Olivella

E Formation of words 2

1 España – *Spain*

In Spanish, an **e** is often put before the combination of **s** + another consonant.
What are the following in Spanish?

station   study
state   student

2 What do the following mean?

esquiar   especial   estómago

3 When you learn a new language, other languages you know are often useful. You
can understand words you have never seen in Spanish before.

Estrasburgo   estadio   estéril
Esteban   esqueleto   estricto
estúpido   estadísticas   espontáneo
escuela   estatua

30 Tiempo libre

A Libro de textos, p. 63 ('¿Qué hacen ...?')

B Libro de textos, p. 63 ('¿Qué hace usted ...?')

C ¿Qué haces en tu tiempo libre?

Unos jóvenes de Toledo contestan a la encuesta.

Split up into four groups. Each group is responsible for an interview. All the members of a group describe and say something about the person chosen by the group. Then put yourselves into cross-groupings, four people in each, and talk to each other, listen to each other and make notes. The aim is for everyone to be able to describe all four young people.

1 Me llamo Rosa Nieto y tengo 16 años. Soy muy aficionada a la música. He tocado el piano durante más de ocho años y ahora he empezado con la trompeta. Me gusta mucho.
Toco en una orquesta que hay aquí en Toledo, "Los Toledanos".
En mi tiempo libre no hago nunca otra cosa.

soy aficionado a –
I am fond of, keen on

2 Me llamo Mercedes Sosa y tengo 17 años. En mi
tiempo libre practico casi siempre
un deporte. Soy muy aficionada al baloncesto
y juego en el equipo del colegio.
A veces, los fines de semana, voy de excursión con
un grupo de amigos. Además me gusta mucho leer.

*el colegio – private
secondary school*

3 Me llamo Carlos Sanjuán. Tengo 18 años.
Trabajo en una tintorería. Después del trabajo,
dos días a la semana, voy a una academia
de lenguas. Estudio inglés. Tengo que estudiar
en casa también. Por eso no tengo
mucho tiempo libre. A veces juego al fútbol
con los amigos del barrio.

*la tintorería – dry-
cleaner's*
a la semana – per week
*la academia de lenguas –
language school*
por eso – therefore
el barrio – district

4 Me llamo Mateo Hierro. Tengo 16 años. Colecciono
sellos y escribo a mucha gente del extranjero.
Escribo unas ocho, nueve cartas a la semana.
Y recibo muchas. Esta semana han llegado tres
de los Estados Unidos y una de Holanda.
Además toco un poco la guitarra. Ah, y los domingos
voy al cine. Bueno, si tengo dinero.

el extranjero – abroad

recibir to receive

D Cuente. (1)

Make up what the three other young people in the photo might say about
themselves.
'*Me llamo . . .*'

E Adjectives · ¶ 8

¿Cuáles son las cualidades que más admira usted en una persona?
Which qualities do you most admire in a person?

| guapo | alegre |

| simpático | valiente | serio |

| generoso | trabajador |

| atlético | ambicioso | inteligente |

Él tiene que ser   **Ella** tiene que ser

_____   _____

_____   _____

_____   _____

What other words would you like to use?
Write them down in English and then try to find them in the dictionary.

F Escuche.

¿Qué cuenta la señora?
'Se llama . . .'

G Cuente. (2)

Describe yourself (name, age, interests, etc.).

31 Sobre gustos no hay nada escrito

A Libro de textos, p. 64 ('¿Qué frases . . .?')

B Libro de textos, p. 64 ('¿Qué opina usted del cuadro?')

C Escuche.

¿Qué sabe usted de Dalí? Complete el texto.

El excéntrico pintor Salvador Dalí (Figueras, Gerona 1904)

es con Picasso y Miró uno de los artistas [1] _____ más

famosos del [2] _____ . Ha pintado [3] _____

cuadros, ha escrito varios ⁴_____ y ha producido

⁵_____, "Un perro ⁶_____"

con el director de ⁷_____ Luis Buñuel.

Federico García Lorca, ⁸_____ del pintor,

⁹_____ un poema titulado "Oda a Salvador Dalí".

Dalí ¹⁰_____ en su vida muchos amigos pero

¹¹_____ muchos enemigos.

Los enemigos de Dalí dicen que en realidad ha tenido sólo

un amigo: ¹²_____.

VOCABULARIO

excéntrico, -a *eccentric*
el pintor *painter*
varios, -as *several*
el director *director*
el poema *poem*
titulado, -a *entitled*
una oda *ode*
el enemigo *enemy*
en realidad *really and truly*

D Adjectives · ¶ 8, 9

Which adjectives are the opposite of each other?
Write them down in two columns.

grande nuevo bueno
feo caro pequeño
largo viejo
divertido corto
bonito aburrido
barato malo

Show that you know what the adjectives mean by writing sentences in Spanish,
including at least one example from each matching pair.

32 Liquidación

Before p. 67

A The demonstrative pronoun **este** · ¶ 28 A

- Write out the correct form of *este* with the following words:

1 _____ casa

5 _____ cuadros

2 _____ país

6 _____ películas

3 _____ ciudad

7 _____ coche

4 _____ libros

- What do *este* and *esta* mean in the following expressions?

este año 8_____

esta semana 9_____

este domingo 10_____

B Regular comparison of adjectives · ¶ 10 A

- Traduzca al inglés:

Las patillas un poco más cortas ...
La obra más importante ...
Las más famosas pirámides ...

- Learn the comparison of adjectives (¶ 10).

- Traduzca al español:

Ana Look, I've found a cheap skirt. Only 690 pesetas. Do you like it?

Julia Yes, but I've bought a cheaper skirt, 590 pesetas.

Ana Really? Let's see. Yes, it's very nice.

Julia I've bought two blouses as well, one white and the other blue.

Ana The blue blouse is the nicest.

Julia Of course. It's the dearest, too.

After the dialogues on p. 67

C Libro de textos, p. 67 ('Compre ropa.')

33 Unas botas de cuero . . .

A Libro de textos, p. 68 ('Conteste a las preguntas.')

. . . y un jersey de lana

B Libro de textos, p. 69 ('Conteste a las preguntas.')

C Ropa

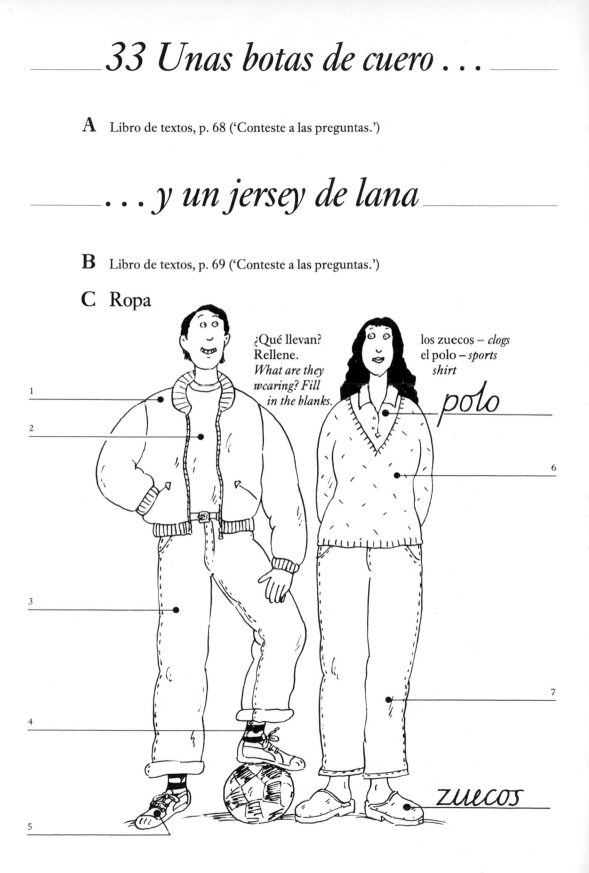

¿Qué llevan?
Rellene.
What are they wearing? Fill in the blanks.

los zuecos – *clogs*
el polo – *sports shirt*

1

2

3

4

5

6

7

polo

zuecos

D En la zapatería

El dependiente/La dependienta	*El/la cliente*
Ask what the customer wants.	
	Ask if there are any white shoes at sale price.
Ask the customer what size.	
	Say what size you take.
Repeat the size. Show the customer a pair of shoes. Say they are leather and very good.	
	Say that you like them. Ask what they cost.
Say they are very cheap. They cost only 1,999 pesetas.	
	Say that's rather expensive. Ask if they have any cheaper shoes.
Reply that these are the cheapest you have. Ask the customer whether he/she would like to try them on.	
	Try on the shoes. Say they suit you very nicely and you will take them (*ellos*). Check the price with the sales assistant.
Repeat the price. Tell the customer to pay at the desk.	

Make up some dialogues of your own. Buy several pairs of shoes, or some clothes.

E ¡Récords! · ¶ 10 A

Rellene con la forma correcta del adjetivo al margen.

La carretera ¹_____ del mundo es la
Panamericana (de Alaska al sur de Chile), que tiene 27 387
kilómetros.   *longest*

El azafrán es una de las especias ²_____   *dearest*
(Un gramo, ¿ cuánto cuesta?).

El estadio cubierto ³_____ del mundo   *largest*
es el estadio Azteca, en Ciudad de México.

El salto de agua [4]_____ del mundo está *highest*
en Venezuela.

El pueblo con el nombre [5]_____ está *shortest*
en Francia. Se llama "Y".

Los [6]_____ consumidores de café son *biggest*
los suecos.

El precio [7]_____ pagado por un cuadro *highest*
durante la vida del pintor es 420 000 libras.
("Ma mère, ma mère, ma mère" de Salvador Dalí.)

A ver si adivina usted el diámetro
del globo de chicle [8]_____ que se ha *biggest*
hecho nunca. (Véase página 120)

(*Libro Guinness de los Récords*)

VOCABULARIO

el azafrán	*saffron*	el consumidor	*consumer*
la especia	*spice*	una libra	*pound sterling*
un gramo	*gramme*	el diámetro	*diameter*
el estadio	*stadium, sports ground*	el globo	*bubble*
cubierto, -a	*covered*	el chicle	*chewing-gum*
el salto de agua	*waterfall*		

F Irregular comparison of adjectives · ¶ 10 B

● Lea y traduzca al inglés:

Una entrevista del instituto Gallup.

El próximo año / ¿mejor o peor que este año?

Mejor	26%
Peor	39%
Igual	22%
No contesta	13%

Base: 1.015 entrevistas

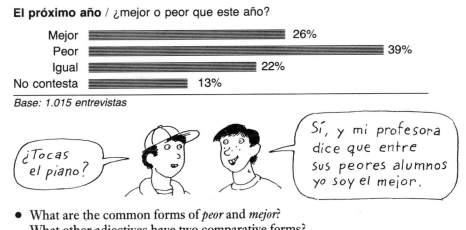

¿Tocas el piano?

Sí, y mi profesora dice que entre sus peores alumnos yo soy el mejor.

● What are the common forms of *peor* and *mejor*?
What other adjectives have two comparative forms?
Learn them by heart and translate the following sentences into Spanish:

1 Pedro is perhaps not the best pupil, but he is the nicest.
2 His elder brother is called Juan. His younger sister is called Luisa. She is nine years old. They live in Madrid. Madrid is the largest city in Spain, but is smaller than London.

34 En el número 85

A Crucigrama

Vertical

1 the week ahead

Horizontal

2 almost
3 until
4 moreover
5 more
6 up
7 still
8 jolly good!
9 one moment
10 towards
11 too much
12 however
13 perhaps

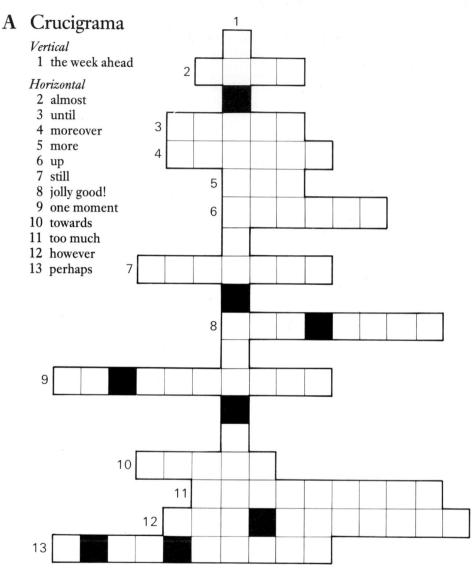

B Traduzca al español

Nearly every Saturday, Soledad goes out with her friends. They never go to the theatre. They nearly always go either to the cinema or to a discotheque. Sometimes they arrange a party at home. Today is Saturday. They are going to have a party at Soledad's. Soledad is making sandwiches in the kitchen. No one has come yet.

At nine o'clock María comes.

'Hello, María.'

'Hello, Soledad. Look, I've brought some records with me.'

'That's good. Ana Mari has telephoned. She's coming soon. She's bringing some records, too.'

(*to arrange* – organizar)

C Libro de textos, p. 71 ('Conteste a las preguntas.')

D Los diez mejores · ¶ 17

There is often a list in Spanish weekly magazines of the ten most popular records.
Make a list of your own. First write down numbers 1–5 in words. When you have
put your favourite records (or books, films, etc.) into order of preference, tell a
friend what they are.

Los diez mejores

1 pr ——————— ———————————————————————

2 ——————— ———————————————————————

3 ——————— ———————————————————————

4 ——————— ———————————————————————

5 ——————— ———————————————————————

6 sexto ———————————————————————

7 séptimo ———————————————————————

8 octavo ———————————————————————

9 noveno ———————————————————————

10 décimo ———————————————————————

35 El piso y los muebles

A   Libro de textos, p. 73 ('Coloquen . . .')

B   **Entre tú y yo 2** (Rooms, furniture, expressions of place)

Trabajen de dos en dos.

A describes the picture on p. 121. B listens and fills in Picture 1 below.
Then change rôles. B describes the picture on p. 122 and A listens and fills in
Picture 2 below.

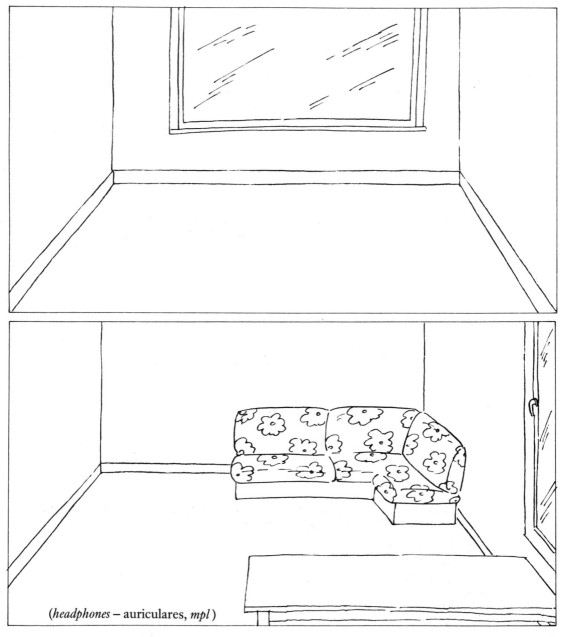

(*headphones* – auriculares, *mpl*)

C Siete errores

Find the seven mistakes in the right-hand picture.
Try to explain what the mistakes are in Spanish. (Think of *hay – está*.)

The Spanish often buy their own flats. Items of kitchen equipment such as cookers, refrigerators, and kitchen cupboards are not usually included in the flat, and the Spanish buy them separately. When they move, they take the kitchen equipment with them.

36 Hogar, dulce hogar

 A Libro de textos, p. 75

B Object pronouns · ¶ 19, 20 B

1 – ¿Dónde pones las tazas?
   ○ *Las* pongo en la cocina.

Replace the following nouns by their object pronouns, as in the example, and choose six different places to put the items.

2 la mesa pequeña
3 las sillas
4 el cuadro
5 la lámpara
6 el televisor
7 los platos

C *No* + object pronouns · ¶ 19, 20 B

1 – ¿Dónde están <u>los platos</u>? No *los* veo.

Continue as in the example. Replace the following nouns by their object pronoun.

2 la lámpara verde
3 los cuadros
4 el televisor
5 la radio
6 las tazas

D Object pronouns + perfect tense · ¶ 20 C

Expand exercise C above.

– ¿Dónde están <u>los platos</u>? No *los* veo.
○ *Los* he puesto en el armario.

Choose where to place the items.

Where is the object pronoun placed:
● with the verb in the present tense?
● with the verb in the perfect tense?
● with the infinitive?
Where is the negative *no* placed?

E Traduzca al español.

– The red chair? Have you put it in the kitchen?
○ No, I've put it in the hall.
– Can you put it in the kitchen? We're going to eat in there.
○ I'm going out now. I'll be back at six o'clock. I'll bring some food then.
– What are you saying? I don't understand.
○ I'm saying I'll be back at six o'clock and I'll bring some food with me. *I'm* going to buy it today.

F En la información

Work in pairs. One works at the information desk in a department store. There is a plan of the store on p. 121.
The other thinks of three or four articles he or she wants to buy, then asks where they are to be found in the store, or where e.g. the bar, the toilet or the telephones are.

Remember to use the words and phrases you know when you ...
● ask something politely
● thank someone
● reply to a thank-you
● are sorry that you haven't got something
● want time to think about it
● think that ...

37 ¿Un buen negocio?

A Traduzca al inglés.

1 hoy mismo
2 en esta misma calle
3 yo mismo

4 hoy día
5 al día siguiente

B Irregular past participles · ¶ 41

Rellene con el participio de
los verbos al margen.
*Fill in with the past participle
of the verbs in the margin.*

La misma noche el jefe le cuenta a su novia:

Esta mañana me han ^{1}_____ dos paquetes,
muy bien envueltos, de uno de mis empleados.

traer

He ^{2}_____ los paquetes en seguida.

abrir

¿Y qué he ^{3}_____?
¡Un plato en dos trozos! ¡Qué tomadura

ver

de pelo! En la tienda han ^{4}_____ los
dos trozos en dos paquetes distintos.

poner

¿Y sabes qué ha ^{5}_____ el tipo? ¡Que

decir

lo han ^{6}_____ por el camino!

romper

C Demonstrative pronoun *aquel* · ¶ 28 B

Fill in the correct form of *aquel* with the following words:

1 _____ libro

2 _____ postal

3 _____ hotel

4 _____ sellos

5 _____ agencia

6 _____ chicas

En el rastro

D Libro de textos, p. 77 ('Trabajen de dos en dos.')

E En la tienda · ¶ 28 A, B

1 Rellene con los pronombres demonstrativos.
Fill in the demonstrative pronouns.

Cliente	¿Cuánto cuesta .... <u>jarra verde</u> que está allí a la derecha?	*that*
Dependienta	<u>15.000</u> pesetas.	
C	¿Y ²........................ <u>plato</u> al lado?	*that*
D	<u>12.000</u> pesetas.	
C	¿No tiene una jarra más barata?	
D	Sí, ³........................	*this*

¿Y ²........................ <u>plato</u> al lado?

Sí, ³........................
<u>jarra pequeña</u> que tengo aquí
cuesta sólo <u>8.000</u> pesetas.
Pero es preciosa. ¡Mire qué colores!

2 Haga usted otros diálogos.

Cambie *jarra verde/15.000 ptas*   *plato/12.000 ptas*   *jarra pequeña/8.000 ptas*

por	vasos grandes/1.500 ptas	jarra/1.300 ptas	vasos pequeños/1.200 ptas
	reloj grande/950 ptas	lámpara/770 ptas	reloj pequeño/650 ptas
	anillo rojo/530 ptas	pulsera/640 ptas	anillo amarillo/390 ptas

F Indirect pronouns · ¶ 22–23

● What does *Le doy 3.000 pesetas* mean?

● Translate into Spanish:
1 Isabel is going to marry José Antonio.
2 She gives him a watch.
3 He gives her a bracelet.
4 Some friends send them a television set.

El Rastro, the fleamarket in Madrid, is in Ribera de Curtidores, and the narrow streets round it. The nearest underground stations are Tirso de Molina, La Latina and Embajadores. It is open on Sunday mornings.

38 *El norte de España*

A Libro de textos, p. 80 ('En las páginas ...')

B Impersonal reflexive construction · ¶ 75

Rellene con la forma correcta del verbo.

1 En la Rioja _____ algunas de los mejores   *are produced*
   vinos de España.

2 En el norte _____ casi la mitad de la leche   *is produced*

   que _____ en España.   *is consumed*

3 En las huertas _____ naranjas, limones,   *are cultivated*
   y mandarinas.

4 La fruta _____ a otros países de Europa.   *is exported*

5 Al año _____ alrededor de 1 700 000   *are exported*
   toneladas de naranjas.

6 Aquí _____ español.   *is spoken*

7 En España _____ muchas lenguas.   *are spoken*

C España

Divide up into groups. Each group reads a separate factual text, i.e.

14 El centro de España
20 El este de España
26 El sur de España
38 El norte de España

Look too at unit 4 (España), and at unit 7 (La capital de España).
After preparation, each group presents its section to the rest.
If possible, use slides, pictures or other material.

39 Un joven gallego

After line 22

A   Libro de textos, p. 83 ('Octavio Ferreira habla de sí mismo.')

B Preterite tense, *-ar* verbs · ¶ 42 A, 43 A

Todas estas personas llegaron a casa muy tarde ayer.
Pregunte y conteste como en el ejemplo.

– ¿A qué hora llegó Pedro?
○ Muy tarde. Llegó a la 1.30.

Pedro	*1.30*
Ana y Carmen	11.30
usted	1.15
el señor Martínez	1.10
tú y Jesús	2.30
tú	3.00

After line 25

C   Libro de textos, p. 84

After line 36

D   Libro de textos, p. 84 ('Cuente lo que hizo ...')

E Preterite tense · ¶ 42 (*regular*), 53 (*hacer*), 54 (*ir*)

Rellene con las formas correctas de los verbos (pretérito indefinido).

Ayer por la noche Juan José Carmena y su

mujer Soledad [1]_____ de un   *volver*
viaje a la capital.

[2]_____ directamente   *ir*
a casa de los padres de Juan José a buscar a sus hijos.

[3]_____ muy tarde a casa.   *llegar*

La hija menor [4]_____ a   *irse*
la cama en seguida.
A los otros Soledad les [5]_____   *preparar*
una tortilla.

Luego [6]_____ café juntos   *tomar*
en la sala de estar y Juan José

le [7]_____ a su hijo   *contar*
mayor algo del viaje.

"Mamá y yo ⁸_____ a
visitar a la tía y a los primos.

⁹_____ con ellos el jueves.

Ayer yo ¹⁰_____ todo el
día con el señor Suárez."

"Y tú, ¿qué ¹¹_____

entonces?" le ¹²_____
el hijo a su madre. – "Yo, pues

¹³_____ en casa de los tíos."

"¿No ¹⁴_____ a El Corte

Inglés? ¿No nos ¹⁵_____ nada?"
"Claro que sí. A ver si adivinas …"

ir

cenar

trabajar

hacer

preguntar

quedarse

ir (tú)

comprar

F Formation of words 3

- Which nouns belong to the following verbs?
(Sometimes there are two.)

estudiar	pescar	nevar
emigrar	comprar	lavar
llover	producir	cultivar
ducharse	gustar	exportar

- Which adjectives or adverbs belong to the following verbs?

descansar	tardar	cortar
casarse	conocer	

- Which other nouns are related to these?

la peluquería   la portería

40 Para estar más segura

A   Libro de textos, p. 85 ('El domingo Beatriz . . .')

B Possessive adjectives · ¶ 31

1   You will have come across many possessive adjectives in the texts. Can you remember what they are? Try to fill in the correct forms.

Almuerzo con ¹_____ familia.   *my*

¿Qué haces en ²_____ tiempo libre?   *your*

Miguel regala las botas a ³_____ hermano.   *his*

Juan volvió a casa y ⁴_____ hermana
nos preparó una merluza.   *his*

Laura le regala el jersey a ⁵_____ hermana.   *her*

¿Qué hace usted en ⁶_____ tiempo libre?   *your*

La familia francesa está en ⁷_____ camping.   *our*

¿A ver si escribís? Un fuerte abrazo de   *your*
⁸_____ sobrino.

Los señores Domínguez no realizaron ⁹_____ viaje a Suiza.   *their*

After correction, learn all the forms.

2   Traduzca al español:

Beatriz and her husband bought the tickets last Tuesday. On Saturday their friend came. His farewell present: three pizzas and a bottle of wine. Without saying anything to his wife, Miguel put the oven on. What a disaster!

C Preterite of *poner* · ¶ 57
Revision of object pronouns · ¶ 19, 20

• Traduzca al español:

1   – Where did <u>Beatriz</u> put <u>the passports</u>?
     ○ I don't know. I think she put them in <u>the oven</u>.

After correction, make up your own variations and practise them.

Beatriz	*the passports*	*the oven*
2 you (*sing*)	the credit cards	the suitcase
3 the boys	the tickets	the cupboard
4 Lola and Carmen	the currency	the handbag
5 you and Luis	the money	the refrigerator

41 En el mercado

After line 4

A Present participle · ¶ 37

Carmen está tomando café. ¿Qué hacen las otras personas?

1 Carmen   2 Ana   3 Pedro   4 Adolfo   5 Paula

6 Luisa y Luis   7 Pablo   8 Raúl   9 ¿Qué tiempo hace?

After line 20

B Expressions of quantity + *de* · ¶ 7

Compre usted mariscos y pescado.

– Póngame <u>un kilo y medio de gambas</u>, por favor.
○ Muy bien. ¿Desea algo más?
– No gracias, no quiero nada más. ¿Cuánto es?
○ <u>405 pesetas</u>.

Gambas 270 ptas

Mejillones 140 ptas

Sardinas 95 ptas

Calamares 250 ptas

1½ kilo	gambas	405 ptas
½ kilo	mejillones	70 ptas
1 kilo	sardinas	95 ptas
½ kilo	calamares	125 ptas

C Indefinite pronouns · ¶ 29 C

Luisa y Emilia están preparando la cena en la cocina.
Pregunte y conteste como en el ejemplo.

melón

cebolla
limón
botella de Rioja

– ¿Tenemos algún <u>melón</u>?
○ No, *no* nos queda *ninguno*.

D Libro de textos, p. 87

E En el mercado

1

El/la cliente	El dependiente/la dependienta
Say good morning. Ask for a kilo of potatoes.	
	Repeat what the customer wants. Ask if he/she would like anything else.
Say you want half a kilo of grapes.	
	Say they are very good, that they are from Almería. Ask if the customer wouldn't like a whole kilo.
Agree and say you will have a whole kilo. Ask if the assistant has any water melons.	
	Reply that you have none left. Say you have some fine melons.
Ask for a little one.	
	Ask the customer if he/she wants anything else.
Say no, that's fine. Ask how much you owe.	
	Say that's 250 pesetas. Say something appropriate when you hand over the goods.
Say something about the price.	
	Say something which shows you agree.
Say goodbye.	
	Say goodbye.

2 Make up your own dialogues. The customer should buy at least two of the
following:

onions	oranges	prawns
tomatoes	mandarins	mussels
green peppers	apples	sardines
olives		squid

F ¿Ser o estar? · ¶ 69–73

Rellene con la forma correcta de *ser* o *estar*.

Trini [1]_____ española.

[2]_____ alta y delgada.

[3]_____ cajera. Trabaja en un supermercado.

Pero esta semana no trabaja, [4]_____ enferma.

[5]_____ en casa. [6]_____ muy cansada.

Tiene un hermano. [7]_____ taxista.

El [8]_____ casado con una madrileña, Victoria,

que [9]_____ muy simpática.

Hoy [10]_____ miércoles. [11]_____ el diez de mayo.
Victoria va a visitar a Trini.

La puerta [12]_____ abierta. Victoria entra.

La sala [13]_____ vacía.

Trini [14]_____ en su habitación. [15]_____ en la cama. *(cont.)*

Victoria	Hola, Trini. ¿Cómo ^16_____?
Trini	Hola, Victoria. Hoy ^17_____ un poco mejor.
	Pero ^18_____ muy aburrido. ^19_____ en la cama todo el día.
Victoria	Sí, pobrecita. Mira, te traigo unas uvas.
	^20_____ de Almería, ^21_____ muy dulces.
	Victoria les prepara un café.
Trini	Oye, mi café ^22_____ muy dulce.
Victoria	Te he puesto azúcar. Si no te gusta ...

G   Palabras y frases 2

After unit 19, you practised words and phrases which are useful in ordinary
speech. Now you will have come across several more.
Try to find what you say when you ...

1   think something is good
2   think that a suggestion is a good one
3   wish to express surprise
4   think that someone has been friendly
5   are slightly irritated and protest
6   want time to think about it (when you address the person with *tú*)
7   want to ask a favour (of someone you say *usted* to)
8   reply that you would be delighted to be of use
9   want to say 'Have a good time' (using *usted*)
10   answer a phrase of that kind
11   think that ...

Por Dios...

Espera.

Igualmente.

¡Qué bien!

Creo que ...

¿De verdad?

Mujer...

Buena idea.

Haga el favor de ...

Hombre ...   Muy amable.

Que lo pase bien.

No faltaba más.

Now try to use some of these words (and those from unit 19) when you play B's
role in Exercise H.

H Conversación

Haga usted el papel de B en esta conversación.
Play B's role in this conversation.

A	B
Oye, Trini cumple 20 años mañana.	
	Show that you are surprised. You ask whether her birthday isn't in August.
No, mañana, seguro. *¿Le regalamos un libro?*	
	Say you think it's a good idea. Ask which book.
Pues no sé, ¿cómo se llama el último libro de Vargas Llosa?	
	Say you don't know.
¿Algo con "muerte", no?	
	Protest; say that that's García Márquez' latest book.
Ah sí, ¿algo con "guerra", entonces?	
	Ask for time to think about it; then say you think it's called 'La guerra del fin del mundo'.
Ah sí, claro.	
	Ask whether A has time to buy the book; explain that you have some errands to do.
Yo sí, sin problema. Lo compro esta tarde.	
	Say that's marvellous.

I Entre tú y yo 3 (Present participle ¶ 37)

Work in pairs. One says what the people in the picture on p. 122 are doing at the moment.
The other listens and fills in a tracing of the picture below.

42 Perú: dos lados de la misma cara

A Libro de textos, p. 90 ('¿Qué fotos . . .?')

B Formation of adverbs · ¶ 11

Many adverbs are formed by adding *-mente* to the feminine form of the adjective.
Example: . . . *concretamente* en el Perú (line 5)
       . . . *realmente* deprimentes (line 9)

- Find the adverbs you have previously come across in the Students' Book (pp. 22, 53, 63, 69, 71, 87).
- Translate them.
- What are the corresponding adjectives?

C Vacaciones

¿Dónde pasó usted sus últimas vacaciones?
¿Qué hizo usted? Cuente.

Si tiene tiempo...

Si tiene tiempo, lea usted estas páginas.
If you have time, read these pages.
In brackets you will find the numbers of the units to which they refer.

Horario 2° BUP (*capítulo 13*) · *página 90*
El español en el mundo (*capítulo 16*) · *página 91*
Dos recetas · *página 93*
   Paella Valenciana (*capítulo 20*)
   Tortilla de patatas (*capítulo 36*)
Dos andaluces en Barcelona (*capítulo 26*) · *página 95*
¿Le gusta leer? · *página 97*
   Elena y María (*capítulo 30*)
   Tres poemas:
   Poema 1 (*capítulo 34*)
   Poema 2 (*capítulo 40*)
   Poema 3 (*capítulo 40*)
Una canción: Desde Santurce a Bilbao (*capítulo 38*) · *página 98*

Horario 2° BUP

Alumno/a: *Laura López y Guzmán, 15 años*

HORAS	LUNES	MARTES	MIERCOLES	JUEVES	VIERNES
9 a 10	Dibujo	Geografía	Inglés	Lengua	Física y química
10 a 11	Geografía	Matemáticas	Lengua	Matemáticas	Lengua
	R	E	C	R	E	O
11₃₀ a 12₃₀	Inglés	Física y química	Latín	Dibujo	Inglés
12₃₀ a 13₃₀	Gimnasia	—"—	Física y química	Latín	Estudio
	T	A	R	D	E
15₃₀ a 16₃₀	Lengua	Latín	Religión	Gimnasia	Matemáticas
16₃₀ a 17₃₀	Matemáticas	Religión	Geografía	Física y química	Latín

El sistema escolar de España

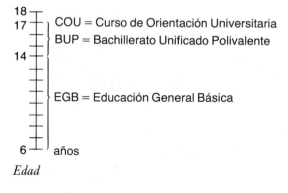

18
17 } COU = Curso de Orientación Universitaria
BUP = Bachillerato Unificado Polivalente
14

EGB = Educación General Básica

6 — años
Edad

Tarea
¿Cómo es su horario?

Vocabulario

history historia
social studies ciencias sociales
biology biología
home economics el hogar
music música
literature literatura
business studies economía de empresa

Vocabulario

el horario *timetable*	la gimnasia *P.E.*	el estudio *study period*
2° = segundo *second*	la lengua *language*	el recreo *break*
el alumno *pupil*	las matemáticas *maths*	el sistema *system*
el dibujo *drawing*	la física *physics*	escolar *school*
	la química *chemistry*	la edad *age*

El español en el mundo

Es la clase . . .
Y todo un coro infantil
va cantando la lección

mil veces ciento, cien mil
mil veces mil, un millón

Antonio Machado, Poesias

GABRIEL GARCÍA MÁRQUEZ
CIEN AÑOS DE SOLEDAD

PABLO NERUDA
20 POEMAS DE AMOR
Y UNA CANCIÓN DESESPERADA

Miguel Angel Asturias
EL SEÑOR PRESIDENTE
NOVELA
LOSADA, S. A

Federico García Lorca
Bodas de sangre
Biblioteca clásica y contemporánea Losada

JULIO CORTAZAR
RAYUELA
EDITORIAL SUDAMERICANA

La literatura en lengua
española es muy rica y variada.

Mario Vargas Llosa,
Perú 1936–
Miguel Angel Asturias,
Guatemala 1899–1974
Federico García Lorca,
España 1898–1936
Gabriel García Márquez,
Colombia 1928–
Antonio Machado,
España 1898–1939
Julio Cortázar,
Argentina 1914–
Pablo Neruda, Chile
1904–1973

MARIO VARGAS LLOSA
LA CIUDAD Y LOS PERROS
NOVELA
PREMIO BIBLIOTECA BREVE 1962

Vocabulario

el mundo *world*	el perro *dog*	va cantando la lección
la soledad *solitude*	la boda *wedding*	*sings the lesson*
el poema *poem*	la sangre *blood*	rico -a *rich*
el amor *love*	la rayuela *hopscotch*	variado -a *varied*
la canción *song*	y todo un coro infantil	
desesperado -a *despairing*	*and a whole choir of children*	

Las lenguas más habladas del mundo

Chino	*846 millones*	Español	*290 millones*	Alemán	*120 millones*
Inglés	*380 millones*	Árabe	*142 millones*	Japonés	*115 millones*
Hindi-Urdu	*295 millones*	Portugués	*141 millones*	Malayo-Indonesio	*106 millones*
Ruso	*295 millones*	Bengalí	*140 millones*	Francés	*100 millones*

(Cifras de 1980)

Hispanohablantes en los Estados Unidos

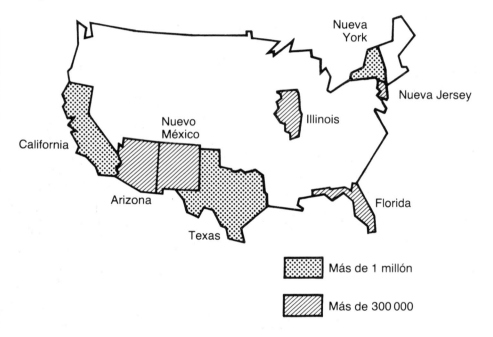

Más de 1 millón

Más de 300 000

El español se habla, además de en España y en América Latina (excepto Brasil y las Guyanas), en muchas partes de los Estados Unidos. (Véase mapa.)

El español se habla también en las antiguas colonias españolas de África y, aunque hoy día muy poco, en Filipinas.

Es una de las seis lenguas oficiales de la ONU (Organización de las Naciones Unidas). ¿Sabe usted cuáles son las otras cinco?
(Solución página 120.)

Vocabulario

la lengua *language*	véase *see*	hoy día *nowadays*
más habladas *spoken most*	hispanohablantes *Spanish-speaking*	poco *little*
además de *besides*		(las) Filipinas *Philippines*
excepto *except*	antiguo -a *former*	ONU *United Nations*
la parte *part*	la colonia *colony*	sabe usted *you know*
los Estados Unidos *United States*	aunque *although*	cuáles *which*
		la solución *solution*

Dos recetas

Paella Valenciana

Hay muchas maneras de hacer
una buena paella.
Hay gran variedad de ingredientes.

Receta para cuatro personas:

Pollo   *uno*
Arroz   *tres tazas de café*
Tomates   *tres*
Mariscos (gambas, calamares,
mejillones)   *medio kilo*
Cebollas   *dos*
Azafrán   *un gramo*
Guisantes   *una lata*
Aceite, sal
(Ajo)
Para decorar:
limón, pimientos

Cortar el pollo en 8 trozos.
Calentar el aceite.
Freír el pollo.
Añadir agua hirviendo (6 tazas de café) y el arroz.
Añadir tomates, cebollas, azafrán, guisantes y sal.
Dejar hervir 20 minutos.
Añadir mariscos, limón y pimientos.
Servir.

¡Que aproveche!

Vocabulario

la manera *way*
hacer *to make*
la variedad *variety*
la receta *recipe*
el pollo *chicken*
la taza *cup*
un kilo *a kilo*
el azafrán *saffron*
un gramo *a gramme*

los guisantes *peas*
la lata *tin*
la sal *salt*
el ajo *garlic*
decorar *to decorate*
cortar *to cut*
el trozo *piece*
calentar *to heat*
freír *to fry*

añadir *to add*
agua hirviendo (f) *boiling water*
dejar hervir *to allow to boil*
servir *to serve*
¡Que aproveche! *Enjoy your meal! (A phrase used by Spaniards at table. The answer is:* Igualmente.*)*

capítulo 36
Tortilla de patatas

Ingredientes para dos personas:
tres huevos
una cebolla
dos patatas
sal y pimienta
aceite

1 Pelar las patatas y la cebolla.

2 Cortar las patatas y la cebolla en rodajas finas.

3 Freír a fuego lento con un poco de aceite.
Echar sal y pimienta.

4 Añadir los huevos batidos.
Freír la tortilla por un lado.

5 Dar la vuelta a la tortilla con la ayuda de un plato.
Freír el otro lado.

¡Que aproveche!

Vocabulario

el huevo *egg*	la rodaja *slice*	añadir *to add*
la pimienta *pepper*	fino, -a *thin*	batido, -a *beaten*
la sal *salt*	freír *to fry*	dar la vuelta *to turn*
pelar *to peel*	a fuego lento *over a low heat*	con la ayuda de *with the help of*
cortar *to cut*	echar *to add, throw in*	el plato *plate*

Dos andaluces en Barcelona

En Andalucía no hay trabajo para todos. Muchos andaluces viven y trabajan fuera de Andalucía, por ejemplo en Cataluña. No todos los andaluces piensan lo mismo de Cataluña. Juan Harillo y Poncio Reyes representan dos opiniones distintas.

Juan Harillo tiene 29 años. Es de un pueblecito de la provincia de Granada. Ahora vive en Bellvitge, un barrio de Barcelona, con su mujer y una hija de un año. Trabaja en el centro de Barcelona, en los almacenes El Corte Inglés. Es conductor. Cada mañana sale de su casa a las siete y toma el autobús para ir al centro. Tarda casi una hora en llegar a su trabajo.

Su mujer, Mari Carmen, que también es andaluza, sale una hora más tarde para ir a trabajar a una fábrica de bolsos. Deja a su hija en una guardería que hay en el mismo barrio. «No me gusta dejarla allí, la verdad, pero ¿qué voy a hacer? El sueldo de mi marido

no nos alcanza. Yo también tengo que trabajar.»

Juan piensa siempre en su pueblo granadino. Le gustaría volver a su tierra. Allí viven sus padres y sus hermanos y allí están sus amigos. No le gusta el estrés y el ruido de Barcelona, la humedad y la

gente. «Los catalanes son bastante antipáticos. Sólo piensan en el dinero. No sé, son muy egoístas. Mire, yo no tengo amigos catalanes. En el trabajo somos andaluces o murcianos y aquí en este barrio sólo hay emigrantes.»

«La vida es muy cara aquí,» añade su mujer Mari Carmen. «Lo único que tenemos es el piso, nada más, ni un coche, ni una moto, nada.»

¿Y el catalán? ¿Lo habla? «¿Yo aprender el catalán? ¿Para qué? No me va a servir de nada. Nosotros estamos siempre con andaluces, con emigrantes como nosotros. ¿Sabe lo que le digo? Sólo hay un idioma en el mundo que me apetece aprender, ¡el árabe!»

Vocabulario

fuera de *outside*	el sueldo *salary, wages*	murciano, -a *from Murcia*
lo mismo *the same*	el marido *husband*	añadir *to add*
representar *to represent*	no nos alcanza *is not enough*	lo único *the only thing*
la opinión *opinion, viewpoint*	*for us*	el piso *apartment*
el pueblecito *little village*	el pueblo *village*	ni ... ni *neither ... nor*
el barrio *district*	granadino, -a *in Granada*	la moto *motorbike*
los almacenes *department*	le gustaría *he would like*	¿lo habla? *do you speak it?*
store	volver *to return*	¿yo aprender el catalán? *me*
cada *each, every*	la tierra *home district*	*learn Catalan?*
salir *to go out, leave*	los padres *parents*	no me va a servir de nada *that*
tarda una hora en *it takes him*	los hermanos *brothers and*	*won't be any use to me*
an hour to	*sisters*	sabe lo que le digo *do you know*
la fábrica *factory*	el estrés *stress*	*what (I'm telling you)?*
dejar *to leave*	el ruido *noise*	el idioma *language*
la guardería *day nursery*	la humedad *humidity*	el mundo *world*
la verdad *(to tell you) the truth*	antipático, -a *unfriendly*	me apetece *I would like (to)*
hacer *to do*	egoísta *self-centred*	el árabe *Arabic*

En el mismo barrio de Bellvitge vive Poncio Reyes. Es también andaluz, de un pueblecito de Almería. Tiene 52 años y lleva más de 20 años en Cataluña. Tiene el título de profesor de catalán y habla un catalán perfecto. Da clases de catalán en un colegio y traduce documentos para un partido político. Con este trabajo no gana mucho, pero a él le gusta ayudar a otros andaluces que viven en Cataluña y no conocen el catalán como él.

«Aquí, si uno quiere trabajar, puede salir adelante. No existe la explotación que tenemos en Andalucía. Y los catalanes, digan lo que digan, son gente seria y cumplidora. A mí me va ese tipo de vida. Yo sé que hay mucha gente que los critica, pero yo le digo mi opinión: aquí hay menos comedia y menos hipocresía que en otras partes.»

(inspirado en un artículo de Cambio 16)

Vocabulario

lleva 20 años en *has been 20 years in*	el partido político *political party*	serio, -a *serious*
tiene el título de profesor de catalán *he's a trained teacher of Catalan*	a él le gusta *he likes (to)*	cumplidor, -a *reliable*
	ayudar *to help*	a mí me va ese tipo de vida *that sort of life suits me*
da clases *he teaches*	conocer *to know*	criticar *to criticize*
el colegio *private school*	salir adelante *to succeed*	digo *I tell*
traducir *to translate*	existir *to exist*	la comedia *comedy (here: performance)*
el documento *document*	la explotación *exploitation*	la hipocresía *hypocrisy*
	digan lo que digan *say what you will*	en otras partes *elsewhere*

¿Le gusta leer?

Elena y María

En Pareja, un pueblo que está al norte de Madrid, viven Elena y María.

«En Pareja todas las mujeres son muy guapas. Elena y María son, sin duda, un buen partido para cualquiera. A Elena le gusta la cocina y a María, los niños. A Elena le gustan los hombres morenos y a María, los rubios. A Elena le gustan los bailes en la plaza y a María, los paseos por la vega. A Elena le gustan los perros y a María, los gatos. A Elena le gusta el cordero asado y a María, la tortilla francesa. A Elena le gusta el café y a María, no. A Elena le gusta la misa mayor y a María, no. A Elena le gusta leer el periódico y a María, no. María prefiere leer novelas (...).»

Camilo José Cela,
Viaje a la Alcarria

Tres poemas

What titles would you give to these short poems?
Read, translate and think before you check their titles on p. 120.

capítulo 34

1
Por las calles
sólo él anda,
nadie más.
Nadie sufre,
nadie ama,
nadie vive
sino él solo.

Pablo Neruda

capítulo 40

2
De la tierra subí al cielo;
del cielo bajé a la tierra;
no soy Dios, y sin ser Dios
como el mismo Dios
me esperan.

Anónimo

capítulo 40

3
Apellídanme rey,
y no tengo reino;
dicen que soy rubio,
y no tengo pelo;
afirman que ando,
y no me muevo;
relojes arreglo
sin ser relojero.

Anónimo

Vocabulario

el pueblo	*village*
sin duda	*undoubtedly*
un partido	*a companion*
cualquiera	*anyone*
moreno, -a	*dark-haired*
rubio, -a	*fair-haired*
el baile	*dance*
el paseo	*walk*
por la vega	*along the banks of the river*
el perro	*dog*
el gato	*cat*

el cordero asado	*roast lamb*
la misa mayor	*High Mass*
preferir/ie/	*to prefer*
la novela	*novel*
Camilo José Cela	*Spanish writer (born 1916)*
andar	*to go, walk*
sufrir	*to suffer*
amar	*to love*
sino	*except*

la tierra	*earth*
el cielo	*sky*
apellídanme	*they call me*
el rey	*king*
el reino	*kingdom*
el pelo	*hair*
afirmar	*to assert, state*
moverse/ue/	*to move*
arreglar	*to arrange, fix, mend*
el relojero	*watchmaker*

Una canción

capítulo 38
Desde Santurce a Bilbao

Desde Santurce a Bilbao
vengo por toda la orilla
con la falda remangada
luciendo la pantorrilla.

Vengo de prisa y corriendo
porque me oprime el corsé,
voy por las calles gritando:
¡sardinas frescu es!

Mis sardinitas
qué ricas son,
son de Santurce,
las traigo yo.

La del primero me llama,
la del segundo también,
la del tercero me dice:
¿a cuánto las vende usted?

Y yo le digo que a cuatro,
y ella me dice que a tres.
Cojo la cesta y me marcho,
¡sardinas frescu es!

Mis sardinitas
qué ricas son,
son de Santurce,
las traigo yo.

El puerto de Santurce

Vocabulario

remangado, -a *rolled up*
la pantorrilla *calf (of leg)*
lucir *to show off*
de prisa *quickly, hastily*
correr *to run*
oprimir *to squeeze, constrict*

el corsé *corset*
gritar *to cry, shout*
"frescu es" = son frescas
  are fresh
la sardinita *little sardine*

rico, -a *good, delicious*
la del primero = la mujer del
  primero (primer piso)
coger *to take up, pick up*
marcharse *to leave*

Unit vocabularies

*, * indicates a word or words which appear in the information panels, pictures, or instructions for exercises.
∣
*

(*m*) masculine noun   (*sing*) singular form
(*f*) feminine noun   (*pl*) plural form

/ie/, /ue/ indicates that the verb takes a diphthong.
See Students' Book grammar section, ¶ 35, 36.

When part of the verb appears, it is followed by the infinitive form. Example: **está** (*estar*).

For some words (e.g. numbers, elements of active grammar) there are references to the grammar section of the Students' Book.

1 América Latina Europa

América Latina (also **Latinoamérica**)	Latin America
¿qué?	which?
país (*m*)	country
es (*ser*)	is it
España	Spain
* **página** (*f*)	page
∣ **cuatro**	four
* **cinco**	five

2 En el aeropuerto

en	in
el	the (*definite article, masc sing*)
el aeropuerto	airport
el avión	aeroplane
para	to
puerta (*f*)	door; *here*, gate
por favor	please
número	number
uno	one
dos	two
tres	three
cuatro	four
cinco	five
seis	six
siete	seven
ocho	eight
nueve	nine
diez	ten

señor (*m*)	gentleman, Mr.
bueno (*m*), **buena** (*f*)	good
día (*m*)	day
buenos días (*m*)	good morning
señorita (*f*)	young lady, Miss
señora (*f*)	lady, Mrs.
¿cómo?	how?
está (*estar*)	you (*sing, polite*) are
usted	you (*sing, polite*)
¿cómo está usted?	how are you?
muy	very
bien	well
gracias (*fpl*)	thank you, thanks
y	and
¡hola!	hello, hi!
¿qué tal?	how are you? how's things?
tú	you (*sing, informal*)
pues	well …
regular	so-so, not so bad
el pasaporte	passport
tenga	here you are
se llama (*llamarse*)	your name is
no	no
me llamo (*llamarse*)	I am called, my name is
soy (*ser*)	I am
de	from
Mendoza	*a town in Argentina*
sí	yes
ah, sí	oh, yes
claro	naturally, of course
* **tarea** (*f*)	assignment, task
* **es** (*ser*)	is he?
* **firma** (*f*) **del**	the bearer's
∣ **titular**	signature

fotografías (*fpl*)	photographs	¿dónde?	where?
información (*f*)	information	el norte	north
llegada (*f*)	arrival	Lisboa	Lisbon
llegadas (*fpl*)	arriving flights	no	not
salida (*f*)	departure, exit		
salidas (*fpl*)	departing flights	el oeste	west
* lavabos (*mpl*)	toilets	el este	east
		el sur	south

3 En la aduana

en	in	la Península Ibérica	the Iberian Peninsula
la	the (*definite article, fem sing*)	la península	peninsula
		ibérico, ibérica	Iberian
la aduana	Customs	limita con (*limitar*)	(it) borders on
		Francia	France
¿qué?	what?	la capital de España	the capital of Spain
hay	is there	la capital	capital
el bolso	bag	en el centro de	in the middle of
un (*m*)	a, an, one	el centro	middle, centre
un libro	book	de	*here*, of
una (*f*)	a, an, one	del = de + el	
una cámara fotográfica	camera	la costa	coast
		ciudades (*fpl*)	towns
algo	something, anything	grande (*m, f*), grandes (*pl*)	large, big, great
más	more		
un momento	one moment, just a minute	como	as
		el País Vasco	Basque country
también	also	la provincia	the province
un periódico	newspaper	Cataluña	Catalonia
una revista	magazine	muchos (*mpl*), muchas (*fpl*)	many
esto	this		
perdón	sorry, pardon	industrias (*fpl*)	industries
un transistor	a transistor radio	Andalucía	Andalusia
		una región	region
el empleado	official, employee	agrícola	agricultural
la maleta	suitcase	exporta (*exportar*)	(it) exports
negro (*m*), negra (*f*)	black	coches (*mpl*)	cars
una camisa	a shirt	maquinaria (*f*)	machinery
una corbata	a tie	productos (*mpl*)	products
bueno	*here*, well	vino (*m*)	wine
ropa (*f*)	clothes	aceite (*m*)	olive oil
blanco (*m*), blanca (*f*)	white	naranjas (*fpl*)	oranges
		mucho	much, a lot of
libros (*mpl*)	books	turismo (*m*)	tourism
botellas (*fpl*)	bottles	sobre	above
¿cuántas? (*fpl*) ¿cuántos? (*mpl*)	how many?	todo	all, everything
		sobre todo	first and foremost
o	or	las	the (*definite article, fem pl*)
tabaco (*m*)	tobacco		
cigarrillos (*mpl*)	cigarettes	las playas	beaches
paquetes (*mpl*)	packets	el Mediterráneo	the Mediterranean
		las Islas Canarias	the Canary Islands
* escuche (*escuchar*)	listen …!	isla (*f*)	island
la cinta	tape		
escriba (*escribir*)	write …!	* falo galego	*Galician:* I speak Galician
* el diálogo	dialogue		
		euskera mintzatzen det	*Basque:* I speak Basque
		parlo català	*Catalan:* I speak Catalan

4 España

		hablo (*hablar*)	I speak
		* castellano (*m*)	Spanish, Castilian
está (*estar*)	(it) is (*of a place*)	la lengua	language
		oficial	official
		el estado	state

español, española	Spanish
el Estado español	the Spanish state, Spain
se hablan (*hablar*)	are spoken
además	in addition
el gallego	Galician (the language)
el vascuence	Basque (the language)
el euskera	Basque (the language)
el catalán	Catalan (the language)
entre	between
pequeño, pequeña	small, little
* **conteste a** (*contestar*)	reply to ...!, answer ...!
las preguntas	questions
están (*estar*)	(they) are
rellene (*rellenar*)	fill in!
el texto	text
* **el libro de ejercicios**	workbook, activity book
* **once**	eleven

5 Al centro

a	to
al = a + el	
el centro	centre
vas (*ir*)	you (*sing*) go; *here*, are you going to?
voy (*ir*)	I go; *here*, I am going to
la oficina	office
adiós	goodbye
hasta	until, till
mañana	tomorrow
¡hasta mañana!	see you tomorrow
el/la taxista	taxi-driver
taxi (*m*)	taxi
una parada	stop
autobús (*m*)	bus
¿adónde?	where? (to where?)
va (*ir*)	goes
la terminal	air terminal
amarillo, amarilla	yellow
lejos	far, far away
cerca (*de*)	near, close
allí	there
enfrente	opposite
* **doce**	twelve
va en autobús	goes by bus
la Plaza (de) Colón	Columbus Square
plaza (*f*)	square
Colón *Christopher Columbus (1451–1506), seafarer to whom the discovery of America is ascribed (1492)*	
cerca de allí	near there
la estación	station
toma (*tomar*)	(he) takes
el metro	the underground
para	in order to

ir	to go
la pensión	guest-house, boarding-house
* **entrada** (*f*)	entrance
* **trece**	thirteen

6 En el centro de la ciudad

de	of
la ciudad	city, large town
va a pie	goes on foot
pie (*m*)	foot
la calle	street
Lope de Vega *Spanish poet and dramatist (1562–1635)*	
la calle Lope de Vega	Lope de Vega Street
lleva (*llevar*)	he carries, is carrying
busca (*buscar*)	he is looking for
un hotel	hotel
un restaurante	restaurant
un bar	bar
una farmacia	chemist's
pero	but
la esquina	street-corner
un grupo	group
una persona	person
pregunta (*preguntar*)	(he) asks
contesta (*contestar*)	(he) replies, answers
un chico; una chica	boy; girl
sé (*saber*)	I know
pregunte (*preguntar*)	ask ...!
* **catorce**	fourteen
entra (*entrar*)	(he) goes in, enters
el farmacéutico	chemist
tarde (*f*)	afternoon
buenas tardes	good afternoon
desea (*desear*)	do you wish, require, want?
aquí	here
por aquí	roundabout here, hereabouts
la calle (de) Cervantes	Cervantes Street
Cervantes *Miguel de Cervantes, Spanish author (1547–1616); wrote Don Quixote*	
un cliente	customer, client
hombre (*m*)	man, human being
no, hombre, no	oh, no; heavens, man!
el hostal	boarding-house, guest-house
que	that, which
la plaza (de) Santa Ana	St Anne's Square
entre	between
el teatro	theatre
la papelería	stationer's
muchas gracias	thank you very much
de nada	you're welcome, don't mention it
* **quince**	fifteen

7 La capital de España

la capital	capital
más de	more than, over
con	with
un millón	million
habitante (*m*)	inhabitant
la ciudad más grande de España	largest city in Spain
las	the (*definite article, fem pl*)
como	as
todos (*mpl*), todas (*fpl*)	all, every
grande	large, big, great
tráfico (*m*)	traffic
los	the (*definite article, masc pl*)
el coche	car
casi	nearly, almost, hardly
avanzan (*avanzar*)	(they) move forward
* dieciséis	sixteen
están (*estar*)	(they) are (*of place*)
el ministerio	ministry
principal	foremost, main
la oficina del estado	state department, office
por eso	therefore
un español	a Spaniard
buscan (*buscar*)	they seek, look for
trabajo (*m*)	work
son (*ser*)	they are
un emigrante	emigrant
los alrededores	suburbs, outskirts
un barrio	quarter, district, area
moderno, moderna	modern
por ejemplo	for example
* diecisiete	seventeen

8 Una individual sin ducha

la individual	single room
sin	without
la ducha	shower
el/la recepcionista	receptionist
la habitación	room
el lavabo	toilet
lo siento	I'm sorry
sólo	only
está bien	*here*, that's fine, all right
para	for
el día	day
la semana	week
muy bien	very well
a ver	let me see, let's see
hoy	today
(el) lunes	(on) Monday
(el) martes	(on) Tuesday
hasta	until
(el) domingo	(on) Sunday
entonces	then
su	your (*polite*)
el nombre	name
la llave	key
necesito (*necesitar*)	I need
el carnet de identidad	identity card
mi	my
11–20	*see* ¶ *14*
miércoles (*m*)	Wednesday
jueves (*m*)	Thursday
viernes (*m*)	Friday
sábado (*m*)	Saturday
* el mes	month
mayo	May
hab. = habitación	room
no. = número	number
Sres. = señores	Mr and Mrs
Sr. = señor	Mr
* Sra. = señora	Mrs
* reserve (*reservar*)	reserve …!
trabajen (*trabajar*)	work …!
de dos en dos	in pairs, in twos
* doble	double

9 En casa de los Gómez

en casa (de)	at home (with)
la casa	house, home
los Gómez ¶ *5B*	the Gómez family
cuando	when
termina (*terminar*)	she finishes
su	her
el trabajo	work
antes de	before
antes de ir	before going
a casa	home
pasa por (*pasar*)	she goes into, 'pops into'
el quiosco	kiosk
compra (*comprar*)	(she) buys
la tarde	afternoon, evening
el periódico de la tarde	evening paper
la madre	mother
la cocina	kitchen
español, española	Spanish
ella	she
trabaja (*trabajar*)	(she) works
la hermana mayor	older sister
la hermana, el hermano	sister, brother
el padre	father
están (*estar*)	(they) are at home
no … todavía	not … yet
llegan (*llegar*)	they arrive, come
tarde	late
más tarde	later
la cajera, el cajero	cashier

el supermercado	supermarket
otro, otra	another
porque	because
estar	*here,* to sit
todo, toda	all
la caja	till, cashdesk
aburrido, aburrida	dull, boring
hace (*hacer*)	does he do?
el/la oficinista	office worker
la compañía de seguros	insurance company
preparan (*preparar*)	(they) prepare
la cena	dinner, evening meal
cenan (*cenar*)	they eat dinner
juntos, juntas	together
el comedor	dining-room
la sopa	soup
la tortilla	omelette
la patata	potato
mientras	while
miran (*mirar*)	they look at, watch
la televisión	television
el televisor	television set
el rincón	corner
del = de + el	
largo, larga	long
estrecho, estrecha	narrow
la mesa	table
la silla	chair
la librería	bookcase
la ventana	window
el reloj	clock
unos, unas	some
la foto(grafía)	photo(graph)
la familia	family
* describa (*describir*)	describe ...!
* sabe (*saber*)	you know

10 Después de cenar...

después de	after
cenar	to have dinner
después de cenar	after they have eaten dinner
el anuncio	advertisement
nuevo, nueva	new
para	for
necesitamos (*necesitar*)	we need
la joven, el joven	young girl, young man
"Necesitamos una joven"	'young girl wanted'
pagan (*pagar*)	they pay
mal	badly
si	if, to be sure
ahora	now
el super = el supermercado	supermarket
ya	already
gano (*ganar*)	I earn

eso sí	of course
trabajas (*trabajar*)	you (*sing*) work
más	more
la hora	hour
la chica	girl
de buena presencia	*here,* with a smart and attractive appearance
¡uf!	ugh!
¡qué machistas!	what male pigs!
la oferta	offer
interesante	interesting
¿por qué?	why?
miráis (*mirar*)	you (*pl*) look
El País	*a major daily newspaper*
20–99	*see ¶ 14*
mil	thousand
cero	zero, nought

Ofertas de empleo

* la oferta	offer
el empleo	job, post, position
ofertas de empleo	'situations vacant'
el dinero	money
hablar	to speak
Ud. (*also* Vd.) = usted	
el inglés	English (*the language*)
norteamericano, norteamericana	North American
urgentemente	urgently
el jefe	boss, head, chief
la venta	sale
el jefe de ventas	sales manager
provincias	provinces
la exportación	export
americano, americana	American
el apartado	postbox (+ number)
el teléfono	telephone
la experiencia	experience
llamar	to ring, call, phone; *here,* ring ...!
preguntar por	to ask for; *here,* ask for ...!
ptas = pesetas	
la peseta	peseta
al mes	a month, per month
libre	free
días laborables	weekdays, workdays
de 8 a 10 de la mañana	between 8 and 10 in the morning
la mañana	morning
el profesor	teacher
las matemáticas	mathematics
la clase	lesson, class
a la semana	a week, per week
* de 4 a 6 de la tarde	between 4 and 6 in the afternoon

11 ... van al cine

van (*ir*)	they go
el cine	cinema
ir al cine	to go to the cinema
¿qué hora es?	what's the time?
medio, media	half
son las nueve y media	it's half-past nine
¿vamos?	shall we go? are we going?
vamos (*ir*)	we go, we're going
Merche	*nickname for Mercedes*
vais (*ir*)	are you (*pl*) going?
la tele	television
dan (*dar*)	they give
Pero si en la tele dan ...	But on television they're showing ...
la película (*also* el film, el filme)	film
¿quién?	who?
mujer	*here*, but, my dear
la mujer	woman
famoso, famosa	famous
el actor	actor
americano, americana	American
la mamá	mother, mummy
* to er mundo e güeno (*Andalusian dialect*) = todo el mundo es bueno	
todo el mundo	the whole world, everyone
el mundo	world
bueno, buena	*here*, nice, kind
¡esa España tan divertida!	how amusing Spain is!
* divertido, divertida	funny, entertaining

12 En el Paseo del Prado

el paseo	avenue, broad street
el Prado	*world famous museum of art in Madrid*
el paseo del Prado	*avenue in Madrid by the Prado Museum*
son (*ser*)	*here*, costs, that'll be ...
¿no?	doesn't it? won't it? *etc.*
el vendedor	seller, salesman, vendor
eso es	that's it, that's right
tiene (*tener*)	you (*polite*) have
el cambio	change (*money*)
tengo (*tener*)	I have
quinientos, quinientas	five hundred
déme (imperative of *dar*)	may I have (*i.e.*, give me!) (*with* usted)
quedar	to remain, be left

no quedan	there are none left
pues	oh, well
¿cuánto?	how much?
¿cuánto es?	how much is that?
ciento, cien ¶ 14	hundred
en total	altogether, in sum
mire (*mirar*)	look! *here*, look here!
doscientos, doscientas	two hundred
trescientos, trescientas	three hundred
cuatrocientos, cuartrocientas	four hundred
* compre usted (*comprar*)	buy ...!
¿cuántos años tenéis? ¶ 68	how old are you? (*pl*)
el año	year
tenéis (*tener*)	have you (*pl*)?
yo	I
él	he
tienes (*tener*)	have you (*sing*)?
si	if
adivinar	to guess
menos	less, fewer
nosotros, nosotras	we
vosotros, vosotras	you (several people whom you address as *tú*)
ellos, ellas	they
ustedes	you (several people whom you address as *usted*)

13 Los meses del año

el mes	month
enero	January
febrero	February
marzo	March
abril	April
mayo	May
junio	June
julio	July
agosto	August
septiembre	September
octubre	October
noviembre	November
diciembre	December
¿cuándo?	when?
el santo	saint
el día de mi santo	name-day, saint's day
antes	earlier, before
vaya	well, I say, I never
¡felicidades!	congratulations
la felicidad	happiness
oye (imperative of *oír*)	listen, hey you!
la fecha	date
el cumpleaños	birthday

pasado mañana	the day after tomorrow
primer, primero (m) ¶ 17	first
el día de clase	school day

Primer día de clase

el profesor, la profesora	teacher
presente	present
ser	to be
sois (ser)	you (pl) are
el hermano	brother
somos (ser)	we are
el primo, la prima	cousin
enfermo, enferma	sick, ill
eres (ser)	you (sing) are
el italiano, la italiana	Italian, person from Italy
el catalán, la catalana	Catalan, person from Catalonia
* si tiene tiempo	if you have time
* el tiempo	time

14 El centro de España

la llanura	plain
la Meseta	the Meseta, the plateau covering the whole of central Spain
ocupar	to take up, fill, occupy
el 40% (por ciento)	40% (per cent)
el territorio	territory
el sureste	south-east
la Mancha	plain in central Spain
la tierra	land, earth
seco, seca	dry
pocos, pocas	few
el árbol	tree
extenso, extensa	widespread, extensive
el cultivo	cultivation, crop
el trigo	wheat
* todavía	still
el molino	mill
molinos de viento	windmills
el embalse	dam
el puerto	mountain pass
la pista	ski-slope
la telesilla	ski-lift (sitting)
el telesquí	ski-lift (standing)
* el telebaby	child-lift

página 31

* en el siglo XVI (dieciséis)	in the 1500s, in the sixteenth century
el siglo	century
el artista	artist

Castilla	Castile, the then kingdom in Central Spain
cultural	cultural
El Greco	painter (1541–1614)
el autor	author, originator
el cuadro	picture
"El caballero de la mano al pecho"	'The Nobleman with his Hand on his Chest'
pintar	to paint
Toledo	town in central Spain, approx. 70 km south-west of Madrid
Valladolid	town, situated approx. 160 km north-west of Madrid
castellano, castellana	Castilian, of Castile
más	here, the most
la empresa	firm
el trabajador	worker
impresionante	impressive, imposing
el acueducto	aqueduct
romano, romana	Roman
viejo, vieja	old
* Ávila	town situated approx. 100 km north-west of Madrid

15 Salamanca

Salamanca	famous university city in western Spain
San(to), Santa	Saint
San Vicente	Saint Vincent
la orilla	bank, shore (of river, lake, sea)
a orillas de	on the banks of
el río	river
detrás (de)	behind
la catedral	cathedral
viejo, vieja	old
el siglo	century
el siglo XII (doce)	1100s, twelfth century
el siglo XVI (dieciséis)	1500s, sixteenth century
la oficina de correos	post office
el correo	post, mail
el buzón	post-box, letter-box
delante (de)	in front (of)
a la derecha (de)	to the right (of), on the right (of)
Correos = la oficina de correos	post office
la librería	bookshop
a la izquierda (de)	to the left (of), on the left (of)
el viaje	journey
la agencia de viajes	travel bureau, agency
el banco	bank
la bicicleta	bicycle
don ¶ 2A	Mr, used before male first names

es de don Julián	it belongs to don J; it is don J's
el dueño, la dueña	owner
uno ¶IC	one
pequeño, pequeña	small, little
¡vaya coche!	what a car!
¿de quién?	whose?
el director del banco	bank manager
el director	director, manager
* el dibujo	drawing, picture

En Correos

el sello	stamp
la carta	letter
menos	minus, less
el cuarto	quarter
las tres menos cuarto	a quarter to three

16 Librería papelería

alto, alta	tall
delgado, delgada	slim
siempre	always
la boina	beret
las gafas	glasses, spectacles
grueso, gruesa	thick
el local	premises
enorme	enormous, huge, vast
la carpeta	file cover
el lápiz	pencil
la postal	postcard
el sobre	envelope
el alumno	pupil
el instituto	State secondary school
el plano	plan, town-map
la clase	lesson, class
la geografía	geography
¿cuánto vale?	what does it cost?
el que	the one that, which
caro, cara	expensive, dear
otros, otras	others
al lado (de)	beside, at the side (of)
el lado	side
la escalera	stairs, staircase
cuesta (costar)	(it) costs
¡estupendo!	excellent! great!
estupendo, estupenda	excellent, marvellous
el bolígrafo	ballpoint (pen)
debajo (de)	under, beneath, below
barato, barata	cheap, inexpensive
bastante	quite, rather
el color	colour
azul	blue
rojo, roja	red
nada	nothing
está bien	that's fine, that'll do
toma (imperative of tomar)	here you are (using tú)
*la concha	shell

17 Desayuno en la cafetería

el desayuno	breakfast
la cafetería	bar, cafeteria
tomar	to have, eat, drink
el café	coffee
me gusta	I like
gustar	to please, appeal to
mejor	better, here, preferably
el té	tea
la pasta	small cake, pastry
el hombre	man
el precio	price
la lista de precios	price-list
encima (de)	above, over
la barra	bar counter
* la bebida	drink
el café solo	black coffee
la leche	milk
* el café cortado	coffee with a little milk
descafeinado	caffeine-free
* el limón	lemon
* el chocolate	chocolate
* el jugo	juice
* el refresco	soft drink
* la cerveza	beer
* el agua mineral	mineral water
el bocadillo	sandwich
* el jamón	ham
* el chorizo	hard, red spicy sausage
el queso	cheese
* el salchichón	salami-type sausage
la magdalena	small, sweet bun
la ensaimada	round, croissant-like pastry
el camarero	waiter
la camarera	waitress
manchego, -a	from La Mancha
el (queso) manchego	La Mancha cheese
¡eh!	do you hear?
claro que sí	yes, of course
en seguida	at once, immediately
el fuego	fire; here, light
chico	dear boy! old man!
otro, -a	another
fumar	to smoke
tener que	to have to
pensar/ie/	to think
tu	your
la salud	health
* desayunar	to have breakfast
* mejor	best
el médico, la médica	doctor
el hospital	hospital
por la mañana	in the morning
la mañana	morning
el amigo, la amiga	friend

los dos	both, the two of them
además	in addition
por la tarde	in the afternoon
estudiar	to study
BUP = Bachillerato unificado polivalente	equivalent of first A-level year (cf. Si tiene tiempo, page 90)

18 Un día completo

completo, -a	full, complete
pronto	soon
empezar /ie/	to begin
mismo, -a	same
es que	it is so that, it's like this . . .
distinto, -a	different, distinct
el curso	course
el horario	working hours, timetable
¿verdad?	don't you? isn't that true?
la verdad	truth
¡qué va!	nonsense! rubbish!
cerrar /ie/	to close, shut
el público	the (general) public
a las dos	at two o'clock
terminar	to stop, end, cease
no . . . hasta	not until
la vida	life
¡caramba!	heavens! gracious!
irme (irse)	to leave, go (away)
¡hasta pronto!	see you soon!
¿a qué hora?	at what time?
* la canción	song

19 Una cita

la cita	engagement, date
la profesión	profession, occupation
marcar	to dial (a telephone number)
llamar	to ring, call, telephone
sonar /ue/	to ring, sound
la hija	daughter
el hijo	son
¡dígame! (imperative of decir)	hello! (on telephone)
soy papá	it's Dad, Father
estás (estar)	you are
estoy	I am
claro que	of course . . .
es la una y pico	it's gone one o'clock
almorzar /ue/	to have lunch
guapo, -a	good-looking, beautiful
¡guapa!	sweetheart, poppet!
¿está mamá?	is Mum, Mummy at home?

Londres	London
a eso de las dos	at about two o'clock
las Ramblas	broad pedestrian avenue in central Barcelona
esquina	here, on the corner of
Pelayo = la calle (de) Pelayo	
la mujer	woman, wife
el tiempo	time
ellos, ellas	them
dice (decir)	(she) says
decir que sí	to say yes
primero	first
la comida	food, meal, also lunch
el niño, la niña	child

20 El este de España

las Islas Baleares	the Balearic Islands
unos, unas	approximately, about
aunque	although
el País Valenciano	the Valencia region
valenciano, -a	Valencian, from Valencia
excelente	excellent
gran ¶ 9 D	large, big, great
la parte	part
la población	population
el campo	countryside
en el campo	here, in agriculture
llueve (llover /ue/)	it rains
poco	a little, not much
gracias a	thanks to
el sistema	system
el riego	irrigation
la producción	production
importante	considerable, important
la huerta	'huerta', irrigated, intensively-cultivated area
se cultivan (pl), se cultiva (sing)	are grown, is grown, cultivated
cultivar	to grow, cultivate
la mandarina	mandarin (orange)
la fruta	fruit
se exporta (sing), se exportan (pl)	is exported, are exported
exportar	to export
alrededor de	about
una tonelada	ton (1000 kilos)
al año	a year, per year
produce (producir)	(it) produces
la cebolla	onion
el arroz	rice
el tomate	tomato
el pimiento	green pepper
el mar	sea
el marisco	shellfish
la gamba	prawn
el calamar	squid
el mejillón	mussel
estos, estas	these

el ingrediente	ingredient
la paella	paella (*chicken, rice and sea-food*)

página 42

menos de	less than
total	total
industrial	industrial
pues	then, thus
industrializado, -a	industrialized
la mitad	half
su	its
el servicio	service occupation
el inmigrante	immigrant
catalán, catalana	Catalan, Catalonian
sin embargo	however
en general	in general
el problema	problem
grave	serious, grave
el clima	climate
agradable	pleasant, agreeable
turístico, -a	tourist
e ¶89 E	and
no muy	not very
lejos de	far from
la zona	area, zone
frecuentado, -a	visited, frequented
bonito, -a	beautiful, lovely, pretty
desconocido, -a	unknown
* popular	popular
la calle más popular	the most popular street
desde	from … (*as in:* from Madrid to Seville, from Monday to Friday)
hasta	… to
Plaza de Cataluña (en *catalán:* Plaça de Catalunya)	*large, open square in the centre of Barcelona*
el puerto	harbour, port
venden (*vender*)	they sell, are sold
la flor	flower
incluso	as well as, including
el pájaro	bird
el animal	animal
sagrado, -a	sacred, holy
el corazón	heart
la obra	work (of art)
* el arquitecto	architect

21 De paso por Elche

de paso por	visiting, on the way through
el guía	guide
este, esta	this
la escultura	sculpture
la Dama de Elche	The Lady from Elche
la obra	work (of art)
importante	important, significant
la cultura	culture
ibérico, -a	Iberian
precioso, -a	beautiful, exquisite
la copia	copy
el original	original
el museo	museum
arquelógico, -a	archaeological
la abuela	grandmother
el abuelo	grandfather
tener sed	to be thirsty
la sed	thirst
comer	to eat
podemos (*poder/ie/*)	we can, are able to
descansar	to rest
el rato	moment, a while
quieren (*querer / ue/*)	you want
beber	to drink
saber	to know
vender	to sell
el helado	ice-cream
creo que sí	I think so
creer	to think, believe
mí	me
la vainilla	vanilla
¿no quiere nada más?	don't you want anything else?
no … nada	nothing
así	like this
oiga (imperative of *oír*)	hello there! (listen!)
diga (imperative of *decir*)	what would you like? (say!)
la cerveza	beer
algo de comer	something to eat
el salchichón	sausage
tener hambre	to be hungry
el hambre (*f*)	hunger
que	for
señores	'Sir and madam' – *often not translated*
la abuelita	grandma
enviar	to send
el dinero	money
todavía	still
el duro	five-peseta coin
los diez duros de la semana	the fifty pesetas I got as pocket-money
de aquí	from here
el castellano, la castellana	Castilian, person from Castile
trabajo de guía	I work as a guide
durante	during
las vacaciones	holidays, vacation
el estudiante	student
la medicina	medicine
la universidad	the university
la Universidad Autónoma	*one of Madrid's three universities*
autónomo, -a	independent, autonomous
* la fresa	strawberry
* la nata	cream

22 Llamada telefónica

la llamada telefónica	telephone call
la matrícula	registration, licence plate
alemán, alemana	German
aparcar	to park
la gasolinera	petrol station
las afueras	outskirts
el conductor	driver
sacar	to take out
la guía	guide(book)
su	his
leer	to read
la atención	attention
al fin	in the end, finally
el fin	end
subrayar	to underline
la dirección	address
la mano	hand
el empleado, la empleada	employee
el castellano	Spanish/Castilian (the language)
perfecto, -a	perfect
llamar (por teléfono)	to ring, call, telephone
reservar	to reserve
la cabina	telephone kiosk
la carretera	main road

Guía de hoteles

* la categoría	category, type
el establecimiento	establishment, *here*, name of the hotel
el número	number
el baño	bathroom
la comida	lunch
HR = hotel residencia	hotel
P = pensión	boarding-house, guest-house
el sitio	place, situation
céntrico, -a	central
pintoresco, -a	picturesque
el garaje	garage
el jardín	garden
el aire	air
el aire acondicionado	air-conditioning
la calefacción	(central) heating
admite (*admitir*)	allows
el perro	dog
* oscilar	to vary

Instrucciones

* la instrucción	instruction
introduzca (imperative of *introducir*)	put in! insert!

la moneda	coin
ptas = pesetas	
la ranura	slot
superior	upper
descuelgue (imperative of *descolgar*)	take off . . .! pick up . . .!
el auricular	telephone receiver
espere (imperative of *esperar*)	wait . . .!
la señal	tone, signal
* marque (imperative of *marcar*)	dial . . .!

Llamadas internacionales

* internacional	international
el indicativo de(1) país	international code number
sin	without
el indicativo de población	city or town code number
la población	city or town
seguidamente	immediately, without a break
* el abonado	subscriber
* Alemania	Germany
República Democrática (Alemana) R.D.A.	East Germany
República Federal (Alemana) R.F.A.	West Germany
Austria	Austria
Dinamarca	Denmark
Finlandia	Finland
Francia	France
el Reino Unido	United Kingdom, U.K.
Noruega	Norway
los Países Bajos	the Low Countries, Netherlands
bajo, -a	low
Suecia	Sweden
los Estados Unidos, EE.UU.	the United States, USA
* México (*sometimes spelt* Méjico)	Mexico

23 El tiempo

el tiempo	weather
el sol	sun
hace sol	it is sunny
el calor	heat
hace calor	it is hot

hace buen tiempo	the weather is fine; it's fine weather
llueve (*llover / ue/*)	it's raining
el viento	wind
hace viento	it's windy
malo, mal (*m*) ¶ *9 C*	bad
hace mal tiempo	the weather is bad; it's bad weather
nieva (*nevar / ie/*)	it's snowing
el frío	cold
hace frío	the weather's cold; it's cold

... y las estaciones del año

la estación (del año)	the time of year, season
la primavera	spring
el verano	summer
el otoño	autumn
el invierno	winter
* "en abril aguas mil"	there's a lot of rain in April
el agua (*f*)	water
el campo	field
la amapola	poppy
seco, -a	dry
la uva	grape
maduro, -a	ripe
* suave	mild, gentle

24 En la playa

la playa	beach
hablar	to speak
el español	Spanish (the language)
un poco	a little
Estocolmo	Stockholm
el novio	fiancé
él no	not he
entender /ie/	to understand
francés, francesa	French
el francés, la francesa	Frenchman, Frenchwoman
la barca	boat
nuestro, -a	our
el camping	camping site
¿de verdad?	really?
vivir	to live
desde hace ¶ *40*	for ... years
la gente	people
subir	to go up, walk up
la piscina	swimming-pool
bueno	*here*, O.K.
escribir	to write
es verdad	it's true; that's true
mira (*mirar*)	look! look at this! (using *tú*)

la tía	aunt
* el kiosko (*sometimes spelt quiosco*)	kiosk

25 Dos postales ...

* Sr. D. = Señor Don	Mr (*in front of first and surnames on letters*)
* Espanha	*Portuguese spelling of España (Spain)*
querido, -a	beloved; *here*, dear
ya	now, already
vamos a estar	we shall be
alquilar	to rent, hire
luego	after, since, later
vamos a ir	we shall go
mañana por la mañana	tomorrow morning
regresar	to return
el saludo	greeting
saludos	kind regards
* Srta. = Senorita Mª Ángeles = María de los Ángeles	
* c/ = calle	
¡al fin!	at last!
bonito, -a	pretty; *here*, fine
el cielo	sky
¡qué cielo tan azul! ¶ *10 C*	what a blue sky!
tan	so
el Mediterráneo	Mediterranean
no ... nunca	never
quedarse	to stay
me	me
voy a quedarme	I'll be staying
quince días	a fortnight
recuerdos a	very best wishes to
el beso	kiss
el abrazo	hug

... y una carta de México

México D.F. (= Distrito Federal)	Mexico City
el tío	uncle
queridos tíos ¶ *5 C*	dear aunt and uncle
realmente	really, truly
impresionante	impressive
¡cuánta gente!	so many people!
¡qué tráfico!	what traffic!
unos, unas	about, approximately
imaginarse	to imagine
que	that
medio año	six months
la industria	industry
el petróleo	petroleum, oil
gracias a	thanks to
la beca	scholarship; grant
el gobierno	government

mexicano, -a	Mexican
aprender	to learn
mucho	a lot, a great deal
dentro de poco	shortly, soon
la visita	visit
la visita de estudios	study-trip, educational visit
la plataforma	platform
el golfo	gulf, bay
el fin de semana	weekend
la excursión	excursion, trip
este domingo	on Sunday
donde	where
encontrarse /ue/	to be situated, found
la pirámide	pyramid
la luna	the moon
más adelante	further on, later on
adelante	forward
llamarse	to be called
la broma	joke
el muncipio	town, township
por lo demás	for the rest, otherwise
llevar	to carry, *here*, live
levantarse	to get up
temprano	early
acostarse /ue/	to go to bed
¿qué tal?	how?
la Navidad	Christmas
fuerte	strong, powerful, *here*, big
vuestro, -a	your
el sobrino	nephew
la sobrina	niece
a ver si escribís	*appr.* hope you'll write soon
* Avda. = avenida	
la avenida	avenue
* Felipe II (segundo)	Philip the Second, *Spanish king (1527–1598)*

26 El sur de España

entre otras cosas	among other things
entre	among, between
la aceituna	olive
repartido, -a	distributed, divided up
está mal repartida	it is unevenly distributed
el campesino	peasant
propio, -a	own
por otro lado	on the other hand
el terrateniente	landowner
el latifundio	large country estate
rural	rural
poseer	to own, possess
alguno, -a, -os, -as	some
cultivar	to cultivate
la finca	estate, holding, land
utilizar	to use, make use of
el tractor	tractor

la sembradora	sowing-machine, seed-drill
hasta	even
la computadora	computer
como	as, since, because
el andaluz, la andaluza	Andalusian, man/woman from Andalusia
andaluz -a	Andalusian
encontrar /ue/	to find
emigrar	to emigrate
el extranjero	abroad
quizás	perhaps
la contaminación	pollution
la escasez	shortage, lack
el agua (*f*) potable	drinking water
además de	besides, in addition to
tradicional	traditional
el árabe	Arab
rico, -a	rich, wealthy
los países productores de petróleo	the oil-producing countries
productor, -a	productive, producing
a	to, in order to
pasar	to pass, spend
la influencia	influence
árabe	Arabian, Arabic (*language*)
el monumento	monument
el valor	worth, value
la Alhambra	*Moorish palace in Granada in southern Spain*

página 56

* el interior	interior, inner
el olivo	olive tree
la riqueza	wealth, riches
el olivar	olive grove
entero, -a	whole
la temperatura	temperature
medio, -a	average, mean
15,7° = quince coma siete grados	
* el grado	degree

27 Un campesino

el campesino	countryman, peasant
el soltero	bachelor
el pueblecito	little village
el pueblo	village
la provincia	province
la finca	farm
el cerdo	pig
la gallina	hen
la vaca	cow
todos los días	every day
dar	to give
da (*dar*) de comer a	to feed
el animal	animal

ordeñar	to milk
el camión	lorry, truck
la cooperativa	co-operative (society)
transportar	to transport
a las cinco de la mañana	at five o'clock in the morning
ocuparse de	to look after, take care of
ducharse	to take a shower
pero hijo	but, my dear boy!
afeitarse	to shave
bajar	to go down
la peluquería	barber's, hairdresser's
en la peluquería	at the hairdresser's
acordarse /ue/	to remember
el dentista	dentist
llevar	to take, carry
la cesta	basket
el tomate	tomato
la idea	idea
un par de	a pair, a couple of
el recado	errand
hacer un par de recados	to do a couple of errands
la pila	battery
la radio	radio
la bombilla	light bulb
de 60	*here*, 60 watts
tardar	to be long, be late
el camión no puede tardar	the lorry will be here soon
me parece que	I think that
ponerse	to put on
la chaqueta	jacket
hasta luego	'bye then, see you later

28 En la peluquería . . .

el peluquero	hairdresser
te	you
¡cuánto tiempo sin verte!	it's been a long time! I haven't seen you for ages!
he (*haber*)	I have
haber	have *as auxiliary verb*
bajado (*bajar*)	come down
ha (*haber*)	she has
venido (*venir*)	come
solo, -a	alone
encontrarse /ue/	to be (*ill, well, healthy*)
¿qué hacemos? ¶ 38 B	what shall we do?
cortar	to cut
¿afeitar y cortar?	shave and haircut?
lavar	to wash
el pelo	hair
no muy	not especially
corto, -a	short
las patillas	sideburns
que	than

. . . y en casa de nuevo

de nuevo	again, once more
te han cortado el pelo	they have cut your hair
han (*haber*)	they have
parecer	to seem, look like
pareces otro	you look like someone else
has (*haber*)	you have
la iglesia	church
de la Iglesia	*here*, by the church
gordo, -a	fat, thick
en la del Gordo	at the fat man's place
encontrar /ue/	to find
unas	*here*, a pair of
las alpargatas	canvas shoes with rope soles
el mercado	market
¿sí?	*here*, oh yes?
¿cómo te ha ido?	how did it go for you?
en	at . . .'s
rápido	fast, quickly
he estado con el tío	I was at my uncle's
contar	to tell, relate
estar en paro	to be unemployed
otra vez	again
la vez	time (*as in* this time, occasion)
en muchas partes	in many places, all over the place
la cosa	matter, business
la cosa está fatal	things are really terrible in that quarter
la suerte	luck
¡qué mala suerte!	what bad luck!
pobre	poor
¡pobres!	poor things!
habéis (*haber*)	you have
hecho (*hacer*)	done
especial	special
hemos (*haber*)	we have
la vuelta	walk round, turn round, trip round
dar una vuelta	to take a walk, stroll
por	through, round
el puerto	harbour
dicho (*decir*)	said
gracias por	thanks for
ha dicho que muchas gracias por	he said many thanks for

29 ¿Qué le pasa?

le	him, her, you
pasar	to happen, go on
¿qué le pasa?	what's the matter with him (her, you)?
parece que	it seems that

le duele la pierna	his leg hurts (*literally:* his leg pains him)
doler /ue/	to hurt, ache
la pierna	leg
¿qué te pasa?	what's up with you?
la rodilla	knee
la cabeza	head
el brazo	arm
el estómago	stomach

30 Tiempo libre

el tiempo libre	free time, spare time
libre	free
la encuesta	enquiry
hacer	to do
los días laborables	on weekdays
entrenar	to train
el equipo	team
el fútbol	football
hago (*hacer*)	I do
el deber	homework
generalmente	generally, usually
dormir /ue/	to sleep
jugar al fútbol	to play football
jugar a /ue/	to play (games)
voy al fútbol	*here,* I go to a football match
escuchar	to listen to
el apellido	surname
la música	music
tocar	to play (musical instruments) (*also* to touch)
la guitarra	guitar
ayudar	to help
mis	my
ir a bailar	to go out to a dance
bailar	to dance
ir a misa	to go to mass
la misa	mass
a veces	sometimes
ir de excursión	to go on an outing
los abuelos ¶ 5 C	grandparents
* el vocabulario	vocabulary, wordlist
el instrumento	instrument
el piano	piano
la flauta	flute
la trompeta	trumpet
la orquesta	orchestra
practicar	to practise
el deporte	sport
el tenis	tennis
el balonmano	handball
el baloncesto	basketball
el volibol	volley-ball
esquiar	to ski
patinar	to skate
nadar	to swim
la actividad	activity

cocinar	to cook food
el ajedrez	chess
la carta	playing card
coleccionar	to collect
la discoteca	discotheque
* ir de paseo	to go for a walk

31 Sobre gustos no hay nada escrito

"sobre gustos no hay nada escrito"	'there's no accounting for tastes'
sobre	about, with reference to
el gusto	taste
escrito (*escribir*)	written
¡qué horror!	how awful!
esto es una tomadura de pelo	this is a great legpull, tease, swizz
¡qué cosa más rara!	what a peculiar thing!
raro, -a	peculiar, strange, odd
¿qué te parece a ti?	what do you think?
ti	you
me encanta	I like it very much
encantar	to delight, charm
genial	brilliant, inspired
feísimo, -a	terribly ugly
feo, -a	ugly
¡qué asco!	how disgusting!
sensacional	sensational
fabuloso, -a	fabulous, fantastic
* la frase	phrase, expression
expresar	to express
positivo, -a	positive
negativo, -a	negative
* opinar	to think, have an opinion

32 Liquidación

la liquidación	clearance sale
la rebaja	reduction, sale price
la blusa	blouse
el jersey	jersey, pullover
la falda	skirt
los pantys	tights, pantihose
el zapato	shoe
los pantalones	trousers
el calcetín	sock
los vaqueros	jeans
el niki	T-shirt
las zapatillas deportivas	sports shoes, tennis shoes
deportivo, -a	sports, sporting
el chaleco	waistcoat
el vestido	dress, costume
el abrigo	coat, overcoat
la cazadora	short, zip-up jacket; sports jacket

más barato que nunca	cheaper than ever
aceptar	to accept
la tarjeta de crédito	credit card
Galerías Preciados	*chain of department stores, found in several Spanish towns*
costar /ue/	to cost
el abrigo más barato	the cheapest coat

33 Unas botas de cuero . . .

la bota	boot
el cuero	leather
como	like
otras muchas personas	many other people
esperar	to wait (for)
la ocasión	occasion, opportunity
la sección	section, department
el caballero	(gentle)man
la sección de caballeros	gents' department, men's department
espera (*esperar*)	wait! (*using: tú*)
rebajado, -a	at reduced price
el plástico	plastic
la dependienta	(woman) assistant
calzar	to wear, put on (*for shoes*)
¿qué número calza?	what size do you take? (*for shoes*)
marrón	brown
probar(se) /ue/	to try on
me van muy bien	they suit me very well
mejor	better
práctico, -a	practical
quedarse con	to keep, retain
después de haber pagado	after having paid
acompañar a *¶ 78*	to accompany, go with
la planta	floor, level (*of stores*)

. . . y un jersey de lana

de lana	woollen
la lana	wool
verde	green
puro, -a	pure
la talla	size (*of clothes*)
en rebajas	in the sales
¿te gusta? (*gustar*)	do you like it?
normalmente	usually, normally
regalar	to give (away) as a present
menor	younger, smaller
el hermano menor	younger brother
demasiado	far too
una semana después	a week later
mayor	older, bigger
el/la peor	worst
la compra	purchase
la peor compra del año	the worst buy of the year

34 En el número 85

el portero	porter, caretaker
el edificio	building
el portero automático	*two-way telephone system connecting each flat with street-door entrance*
el estilo	style
modernista	modernistic, functional
sin embargo	however
la portera	female porter, caretaker, concierge
una señora de edad	an elderly woman
la edad	age
lleva más de quince años *¶ 40*	she has lived for more than fifteen years
conocer	to know
todos los que	all those who, everyone who
en ella	in it
está limpiando	she's cleaning
limpiar	to clean
la escalera	stairs
el repartidor	delivery man
los almacenes	department store
el Corte Inglés	*well-known chain of department stores*
el frigorífico	refrigerator
segundo, -a	second
el piso	floor, level (*of flats*)
hacia	towards
el ascensor	lift
el montecargas	service lift
subir por la escalera	to take the stairs, go up the stairs
no . . . nadie	nobody, no-one
no hay nadie	*here*, there's no-one in
vacío, -a	empty
casarse	to get married
le semana que viene (*venir*)	next week, coming week
venir /ie/	to come
¿dónde ponemos? *¶ 38 B*	where shall we put?
poner	to put, place
la portería	porter's room, lodge
¡Ay, por Dios!	Oh, for God's sake!
¡eso sí que no!	out of the question!
caber	to go, fit in; have, be room for
no . . . ni	not even
el alfiler	pin
los padres *¶ 5 C*	parents
en el tercero	*here*, on the third floor
tercero, -a	third
a lo mejor	perhaps, maybe
miren (*mirar*)	look . . .!

ahí	there
traer	to bring, come with
vengo (venir)	I'm coming
de allí	from there
precisamente	precisely, exactly
alguien	someone, anyone
arriba	up (there), upstairs
salgo (salir)	I'm going out
5° = quinto	fifth
4° = cuarto	fourth
* el notario	notary, solicitor
Doña	Mrs (goes with the first name)
* la planta baja	ground floor

35 El piso y los muebles

el mueble	piece of furniture
el sofá	sofa
el armario	cupboard
la cama	bed
el sillón	armchair
la alfombra	carpet, rug
el aparador	chest-of-drawers
la lámpara	lamp
el vestíbulo	hall
el (cuarto de) baño	bathroom
la sala (de estar)	living-room
el dormitorio	bedroom
la terraza	balcony
¿dónde pongo . . .? (poner) ¶ 38 B	where shall I put . . .?
los, las	them
lo	it, him
la	it, her
* coloquen (colocar)	put . . .! place . . .!
* S.A. = sociedad anónima	Co. Ltd, plc

36 Hogar, dulce hogar

el hogar	home
dulce	sweet
el montón	heap, pile
la caja	box
llaman a la puerta	there's a ring (knock) at the door
¡adelante!	come in!
abierto, -á (abrir)	open
conozco (conocer)	I know
la novia	fiancée
rubio, -a	blond
cuantos más, mejor	the more, the better; the more, the merrier
a	to, in order to
buscar	here, to collect, meet
presentar	to introduce, present

te presento a Anita	may I introduce you to Anita; this is Anita
encantado, -a	delighted (to meet you)
mucho gusto	here, delighted, pleased to meet you
la moqueta	fitted carpet
ponerse a	to begin to, start to
el cuadro	picture
el suelo	floor
la taza	cup
de acuerdo	O.K., agreed
el plato	plate (also dish = plate of food)
no los veo	I can't see them
puesto (poner)	placed, put
el vaso	glass
dice (decir)	he (she, it) says
decir	to say

37 ¿Un buen negocio?

el negocio	deal, piece of business
¿en qué puedo servirle?	what can I do for you? may I be of help?
visto (ver)	seen
la porcelana	porcelain, china
el escaparate	shop window
aquel (m), aquella (f)	that
inglés, inglesa	English
la calidad	quality
gastar	to spend (of money)
algo sí	something similar, something like that
hoy día	nowadays
la jarra	jug
la flor	flower
¿cuál?	which one?
roto, -a (romper)	broken
el mostrador	shop counter
el doble	double, twice as much
haga el favor de	please, be so good as to . . .!
haga (hacer)	do . . .!
hoy mismo	today as ever is, this very day
la oficina central	head office
la Seat	the automobile factory SEAT (Sociedad Española de Automóviles de Turismo) in Barcelona, one of the largest industries in Spain
no faltaba más	certainly
¡qué cliente más raro! ¶ 10C	what a strange customer!
la tienda	shop
el regalo	present
elegante	elegant, grand
sin duda	without doubt
el jefe	boss
siguiente	following
al día siguiente	on the following day
contento, -a	satisfied, happy
recibir	to receive

abierto (*abrir*)	opened
abrir	to open
ofendido, -a	offended, upset
seguro que lo han roto	they must have broken it
seguro	sure, safe
el camino	way, road
patoso, -a	clumsy
ja, ja	ha, ha
yo mismo	I myself
cada	each, every
el trozo	piece, bit
envuelto (*envolver*)	wrapped
matar	to kill

En el Rastro

el Rastro	*the flea-market in Madrid*
¿vale?	is that all right?
¡vale!	it's a deal, O.K.
tome usted (imperative of *tomar*)	here you are
* el tocadiscos	record-player
el disco	gramophone record
la pulsera	bracelet
* el anillo	ring

38 El norte de España

la lluvia	rain
el bosque	forest, woods
el prado	meadow, field
abundante	abundant, plentiful
el ganado	livestock
vacuno, -a	cattle
abundante ganado vacuno	a wealth of cattle
se produce (*producir*) ¶ 75	is produced
consumir	to consume
Galicia	Galicia
Asturias	Asturias
la hortaliza	vegetables, greens
la manzana	apple
la comarca	district, area
La Rioja	*region in northern Spain, famous for its wines*
la ría	deep bay, 'fjord'
la pesca	fishing
primero, -a	leading, most important
pesquero, -a	fishing-
la conserva	canning
el pescado	fish
principal	main
el desarrollo	development
la mina	mine
el carbón	coal
vecino, -a	neighbouring
el hierro	iron

Vizcaya	*province, forming together with the provinces of Guipúzcoa and Álava the region of País Vasco*
actualmente	right now, at the moment
a pesar de	despite, in spite of
económico, -a	economic

página 81

dividir	to divide
los vascos	the Basques
varios, -as	various
gobernar /ie/	to rule, govern
la política	politics, policy
la política centralista	policy of concentrating power at the centre
ha habido (*haber*)	there have been
la tensíon	tension, strain
el gobierno central	the central government (in Madrid)
la periferia	periphery, peripheral areas
especialmente	especially, specially
la lucha	struggle
en ocasiones	sometimes
violento, -a	violent, fierce
la guerra	war
la guerra civil	civil war
a partir de	from ... onwards
los años 60	the Sixties
la aparición	appearance
la organización	organization
revolucionario, -a	revolutionary
E.T.A.	*abbreviation of Euskadi Ta Askatasuna (in Basque: 'The Basque Country in Freedom')*
* Picasso	*Pablo Picasso, Spanish artist (1889–1973), lived and worked for the greater part of his life in France*
el Guernica de Picasso	Picasso's painting, *Guernica*
se prepara ¶ 75	one prepares
la instalación	installation
a dos pasos de	quite near to, i.e. two steps away from
el pintor	painter
inmortalizar	to immortalize
* destruir	to destroy

39 Un joven gallego

gallego, -a	Galician
hacer buen día	to be good weather
¡ojalá!	let's hope so!
lleva ... lloviendo ¶ 40	it's been raining for ...
la bolsa	bag
el termo	thermos flask
la cara	face

tener cara de	to look
cansado, -a	tired
ayer	yesterday
llegó (*llegar*)	he came, arrived
tardísimo	terribly late
llegué (*llegar* ¶ 89 B)	I came, arrived
volvió (*volver*)	(he) came back, returned
la merluza	hake
riquísimo, -a	very tasty
rico, -a	tasty, delicious
lo pasamos estupendamente	we had a marvellous time
pasar	to spend time
estupendamente	fantastic, marvellous
el pueblo	village
situado, -a	situated, which is, which lies
los hermanos ¶ 5 C	brothers (*also* brothers and sisters)
el único	the only
casado, -a	married
emigrar	to emigrate
hace	... years ago
está haciendo (*hacer*)	is doing
el servicio militar	military service, national service
Ceuta *town and military base in northern Morocco, belonging to Spain*	
como	as, since
pescar	to fish

página 84

descargar	to unload
la pesca	(fish) catch
la lonja	(fish) market
subastar	to auction
* la sardina	sardine
menos de	less than
satisfecho, -a	satisfied, content
la venta	sale
irse	to go away, set off
el pescador	fisherman
vimos (*ver* ¶ 66)	we saw
hiciste (*hacer* ¶ 53)	you did
fui (*ir* ¶ 54)	I went
tiene buena mano para la comida	she is good at cooking

40 Para estar más segura

para estar más segura	for safety's sake
seguro, -a	safe, secure
decidir	to decide
por fin	at last, finally
realizar	to carry out, realize
soñar /ue/	to dream
soñado, -a	dreamt of, ideal

el viaje	journey, trip
Suiza	Switzerland
el billete	ticket
dijo (*decir* ¶ 49)	(she) said
nada de ...	certainly no ...
la forma	way, manner
democrático, -a	democratic
de forma poco democrática	not very democratic
las divisas	currency
el franco	franc
recoger	to collect
la gestoría	agency, office dealing with government departments
el ladrón	thief
nos	us
robar	to steal, rob
nos lo roba todo	robs us of everything
la desgracia	misfortune, setback
esconder	to hide
sin decir nada	without saying anything
el marido	husband
puso (*poner* ¶ 57)	(she) put
el horno	oven
la noche	evening, night
por la noche	in the evening
la pizza	pizza
el Rioja	Rioja wine
celebrar	to celebrate
la despedida	farewell, departure
encender /ie/	to light; *here*, to put on
se calentó, se calentó ...	it became hotter and hotter ...
salir	to come out
el humo	smoke
oscuro, -a	dark
un olor a	a smell of
quemado, -a	burnt
la tragedia	tragedy
correr	to run
su, sus	their
la ilusión	illusion, dream
convertido, -a (en)	changed (into)

41 En el mercado

el mercado	market hall
póngame (*poner*)	give me ...!
el kilo	kilo
le pongo buen peso	I'll add a bit over
el peso	weight
amable	kind, friendly
muy amable	very kind of you
la uva	grape
dulce	sweet
algún, alguno (*m*)	any
el melón	melon
no ... ninguno, -a	not one

no me queda ninguno	I've none left
la sandía	water melon
verde	unripe, still green
maduro, -a	ripe
¿cuánto le debo?	how much do I owe you?
deber	to owe
tanto	so much
¡comó suben los precios!	how prices rise!
que lo pase bien	have a good time (using usted)
igualmente	same to you
* la lechuga	lettuce
la pera	pear
* el melocotón	peach

42 Perú: dos lados de la misma cara

las Ciencias Sociales	social sciences
la ciencia	science
el material	material
ilustrar	to illustrate, illuminate
sobre	about
el disco	record
el folleto	brochure, pamphlet
estuve (estar ¶ 51)	I was
concretamente	specifically, exactly
mostrar /ue/	to show
chocar	to shock
la pobreza	poverty
la escena	scene
deprimente	depressing
el poblado	village
indígena	indigenous, native
el poblado indígena	Indian village
los Andes	the Andes
el lago	lake (or the sea)
el indio	Indian
la selva	forest, jungle

el Amazonas	the Amazon river
primitivo, -a	primitive
la vivienda	dwelling
la paja	straw
la escuela	school
el futuro	future
por	owing to, due to
por eso	because of that
el analfabetismo	illiteracy
depender (de)	to depend (on)
la imagen	picture, image
real	real, true
Hispanoamérica	Spanish-America
es cierto	that's right
cierto, -a	sure, correct
hay que	one must, one has to
tener cuidado (con)	be careful (with), be cautious (with)
la generalización	generalization
tratarse de	to be about
continuar	to continue
pasado, -a	previous, last
por Navidad	at Christmas time
pudimos (poder ¶ 56)	we could, we were able to
el piloto	pilot
Iberia	the Spanish state airline
visitar	to visit
el lugar	place
la propiedad	property
el pariente	relation, relative
más que ¶ 10 E	more than
la maquinaria	machinery
moderno, -a	modern
aunque	although
el arma (f)	weapon
el barrio	district, quarter
el/la colega	colleague
elegantísimo, -a	really elegant
el monumento	monument
inca	Inca
la impresión	impression
me llevé (llevarse)	I carried, took away with me
positivo, -a	positive

Supplement to certain exercises

Capítulo 11, ejercicio E. *Adivinanza*

A casa.

Capítulo 12, ejercicio G. *Entrevistas*

You are **B**:

Interview 1

Answer A's questions.

You are called Amalia Carpentier
- are from Madrid
- work for a (north) American firm
- speak English
- earn 80,000 pesetas a month
- work forty hours a week
- go to work by underground

Interview 2

Ask A . . .
- what his name is
- from which town he comes
- what his profession or occupation is
- which languages he speaks
- how many lessons a week he has
- how much he earns
- whether he goes to work on foot

Capítulo 15, ejercicio C. *Entre tú y yo 1*

Picture 1

Picture 2 (capítulo 15, ejercicio C)

Capítulo 33, ejercicio E. *¡Récords!*

48,9 centímetros.

Si tiene tiempo . . . *El español en el mundo*

Las otras lenguas oficiales de la ONU son (por orden alfabético): el árabe, el chino, el francés, el inglés y el ruso.

Si tiene tiempo . . . *¿Le gusta leer?*

Los títulos son: *The titles are:*
Poema 1: El egoísta
Poema 2: La lluvia
Poema 3: El sol

Capítulo 35, ejercicio B. *Entre tú y yo 2*

Picture 1

Capítulo 36, ejercicio F. *En la información*

GALERIAS PRECIADOS

5ª Planta	*Muebles*
4ª Planta	*Cafetería · Teléfono* *Artículos de regalo* *Servicios*
3ª Planta	*Artículos de deporte* *Calzados*
2ª Planta	*Confección señoras —* *caballeros — niños*
1ª Planta	*Librería · Papelería* *Discos Radio TV*
Planta baja	*Hogar* *Comestibles*

VOCABULARIO

el artículo   *article*
el regalo   *present*
los servicios   *toilets*
los calzados   *footwear*
la confección   *clothing*
el disco   *record*
el hogar   *here, household*
    goods
los comestibles   *food*

Capítulo 41, ejercicio I. *Entre tú y yo 3*

English–Spanish vocabulary

See also the *Expressions and Phrases* section in the Students' Book, pp. 92–94.

Numbers: see Grammar ¶ 14.

Months: see unit 13.

Names of Countries: see maps in Students' Book, pp. 4–5 (unit 1).

A

a, an un, una
able: to be able to poder /ue/
about cerca de, alrededor de
above encima de; **above all** sobre todo
abroad el extranjero; **to go abroad** ir al extranjero
to **accept** aceptar
to **accept, receive, be given** recibir
to **accompany** acompañar
to **ache** doler /ue/; **my head aches** me duele la cabeza
actor el actor
address la dirección
advertisement el anuncio
aeroplane el avión
after después de; **after eating** después de comer
afternoon la tarde; **in the afternoon** por la tarde
afterwards después
again de nuevo; otra vez
age la edad
agreeable agradable
air el aire
air-conditioning el aire acondicionado
airport el aeropuerto
air-terminal la terminal
alone solo, -a
all todo, -a; todos, -as
almost casi
already ya
also también
although aunque
always siempre
American americano, -a; norteamericano, -a
among entre; **among other things** entre otras cosas
amusing divertido, -a
and y (*also* e, *see* ¶ 89 E)
& Co. Ltd/plc la sociedad anónima, S.A.
Andalusia Andalucía
Andalusian el andaluz, la andaluza (*person*)
Andalusian andaluz, -a
Andes los Andes

B

animal el animal
another otro, -a
to **answer** contestar
apartment el piso
apple la manzana
Arab el árabe (*person*)
Arab árabe
area la región, el territorio, la zona
arm el brazo
armchair el sillón
arrival la llegada
to **arrive** llegar
art: (work of) art la obra
artist el/la artista
as como
to **ask for** preguntar; to **ask after** preguntar por (*a person*)
assistant (shop) el dependiente
Asturias Asturias
at en
at about (two o'clock) a eso de (las dos)
at ...'s en casa de
at Christmas por Navidad
at last al fin, por fin
at once en seguida
at what time? ¿a qué hora?
to **auction** subastar
aunt la tía
author el autor; la autora
autumn el otoño
avenue el paseo
average medio, -a

bachelor el soltero
bad malo (mal), mala
badly mal
bag el bolso, la bolsa
balcony la terraza
Balearic Islands las Islas Baleares
ballpoint pen el bolígrafo
bank el banco
bank (of river) la orilla; **on the banks of** a orillas de
bank manager el director de banco
bar el bar; la cafetería
bar counter la barra
Basque vasco, -a

Basque Country el País Vasco
Basque language el vascuence, el euskera
basket la cesta
basketball el baloncesto
bathroom el (cuarto de) baño
battery la pila
to **be** estar; ser
to **be** estar; encontrarse /ue/ (*of situation and of health*)
to **be able to** poder /ue/
to **be careful (with)** tener cuidado (con)
to **be forced to** tener que
to **be hungry** tener hambre
to **be thirsty** tener sed
beach la playa
beautiful guapo, -a; bonito, -a; precioso, -a
because porque
bed la cama
bedroom el dormitorio
beer la cerveza
before (*time*) antes de; **before** (*going away*) antes de (irse)
before (*place*) delante (de)
to **begin to** empezar a; ponerse a
behind detrás (de)
to **believe** creer
beret la boina
beside al lado de
best el/la mejor
better mejor
between entre
bicycle la bicicleta
big grande (gran)
bird el pájaro
birthday el cumpleaños
bit el trozo
black negro, -a
blond rubio, -a
blouse la blusa
blue azul
boarding-house la pensión, el hostal
boat el barco; (*small*) la barca
book el libro
bookshelf la librería
bookshop la librería
boot la bota
to **border (on)** limitar (con)

boring aburrido, -a
boss el jefe
both los dos, las dos
bottle la botella
box la caja
boy el chico
bracelet la pulsera
to **break** romper /ue/
breakfast el desayuno
to **bring** traer
brochure el folleto
broken roto, -a
brother el hermano
brothers and sisters los hermanos
brown marrón
building el edificio
bus el autobús
business el negocio
bus-stop la parada de autobús
but pero
to **buy** comprar
by por

C

café la cafetería
caffeine-free (coffee) (el café) descafeinado
cake la pasta
to **be called** llamarse; **what are you called?** ¿cómo se llama usted?
camera la cámara fotográfica
campsite el camping
Canary Islands las Islas Canarias
capital la capital
car el coche
care el cuidado
to **be careful** tener cuidado (con)
caretaker el portero, la portera
carpet la alfombra; (*fitted*) la moqueta
carrier-bag la bolsa
to **carry** llevar
to **carry out** realizar
cash-desk la caja
cashier el cajero, la cajera
Castile Castilla
Castilian castellano, -a
Catalan catalán, catalana
Catalonia Cataluña
catch (of fish) la pesca

cathedral la catedral
cattle el ganado vacuno
to **celebrate** celebrar
central central;
  (= *centrally situated*)
  céntrico, -a
central heating la
  calefacción central
centre el centro
century el siglo
chair la silla
change (*money*) el
  cambio
cheap barato, -a
cheese el queso
chemist's la farmacia
chess el ajedrez
chest-of-drawers el
  aparador
child el niño, la niña
children los niños
china la porcelana
chocolate el chocolate
Christmas la Navidad;
  at Christmas por
  Navidad
church la iglesia
cinema el cine
cigarette el cigarrillo
to **clean** limpiar
client el/la cliente
climate el clima
clock el reloj
to **close** cerrar /ie/
closed cerrado, -a
clothes la ropa
clumsy patoso, -a
coal el carbón
coast la costa
coat el abrigo
coffee el café
  black coffee el café solo;
  white coffee el café
  con leche; **coffee with a**
  little milk el café
  cortado
coin la moneda
cold frío, -a; **it's**
  cold hace frío
colour el color
colleague el/la colega
to **collect** coleccionar
Colombus Colón
to **come** venir
come in! ¡adelante!
company la compañía
company (*business*) la
  compañía, la empresa
complete completo, -a
computer la
  computadora
to **consider** opinar
to **consume** consumir
to be **contained in** caber
content contento, -a;
  satisfecho, -a
to **continue** continuar
to **cook food** cocinar
copy la copia
corner (*inside*) el rincón;
  (*outside*) la esquina
correct correcto, -a;
  cierto, -a

to **cost** costar /ue/; **how**
  much does it cost?
  ¿cuánto es? ¿cuánto vale?
  ¿cuánto cuesta?
counter (*shop*) el
  mostrador
country el país
country dweller el
  campesino, la campesina
countryside el campo
course el curso
of course! ¡claro!
cousin el primo, la prima
cow la vaca
cream la nata
credit card la tarjeta de
  crédito
to **cultivate** cultivar
culture la cultura
cup la taza
cupboard el armario
currency las divisas
customer el/la cliente
Customs la aduana

D

Dad, Daddy papá
to **dance** bailar
dark oscuro, -a
date la fecha
daughter la hija
day el día
to **deal with** tratarse de
dear (*expensive*) caro, -a
dear (*letter*) querido, -a
to **decide** decidir
degree el grado
to **delay** tardar
delicious rico, -a
to **delight** encantar;
  delighted to meet
  you! ¡encantado, -a!
delivery man el
  repartidor
democratic democrático,
  -a
dentist el/la dentista
department (*in store*) la
  sección
department store los
  almacenes
to **depend on** depender
  de
despite a pesar de
to **destroy** destruir
development el
  desarrollo
dial (*a telephone*
  number) marcar (un
  número)
different distinto, -a
to **dine** cenar
dining-room el
  comedor
dinner la cena (*evening*
  meal)
director el director
discotheque la discoteca
discount la rebaja
dish (*of food*) el plato
district la región, la
  comarca

district (*of town*) el barrio
to **divide** dividir
to **do** hacer
doctor el médico
dog el perro
door la puerta
double doble
drawing el dibujo
to **dream** soñar /ue/
dress el vestido
drink la bebida; **soft**
  drink el refresco
to **drink** beber; tomar
drinking water el agua
  (*f*) potable
driver el conductor
dry seco, -a
dull aburrido, -a
during durante
dwelling la vivienda

E

each cada
earlier antes
early temprano
to **earn** ganar
earth la tierra
east el este
to **eat** comer
to **eat breakfast**
  desayunar
to **eat lunch** almorzar
to **eat dinner** cenar
economic económico, -a
elder mayor
eldest el/la mayor
elderly man/woman
  un señor/una señora de
  edad
elegant elegante
emigrant el/la
  emigrante
to **emigrate** emigrar
to **emphasize** subrayar
employee el empleado,
  la empleada
empty vacío, -a
end el fin
to **end** terminar
English inglés, inglesa
enormous enorme
enquiry la encuesta
to **enter** entrar en
entertaining divertido,
  -a
entrance la entrada
envelope el sobre
errand el recado
estate (*farm*) la finca
estate (*large*) el latifundio
evening la tarde; la
  noche; **in the**
  evening por la tarde/
  noche
ever nunca
every todo, -a
every day todos los días
everyone todos, todo el
  mundo; **everyone**
  who todos los que
everything todo
exactly precisamente

excellent estupendo, -a;
  excelente
exchange (*money*) el
  cambio
exercise el ejercicio
exercise book el libro de
  ejercicios
excursion la excursión
excuse me perdón
exit la salida; (*at airport*)
  la puerta
experience la
  experiencia
export la exportación
to **export** exportar
to **express** expresar
exquisite precioso, -a

F

face la cara
family la familia
famous famoso, -a
fantastic fabuloso, -a;
  estupendo, -a
far lejos; **far from** lejos
  de
farewell la despedida
farm (estate) la finca
fat grueso, -a; gordo, -a
father el padre
to **feed** dar de comer a
to **fetch** buscar; recoger
few pocos, -as
fewer than menos de
fiancé el novio
fiancée la novia
field el campo
fifth quinto, -a
file la carpeta
film la película, el film
finally al fin, por fin
to **find** encontrar /ue/
fine bonito, -a; elegante
fire el fuego
firm (*business*) la empresa
first primero (primer),
  primera; **first of**
  all primero
fish el pescado
fish-auction la lonja
fishing la pesca
to **fish** pescar
fisherman el pescador
to **fit in** caber
five-peseta coin el duro
flat el piso
floor el suelo
floor (*level*) la planta
flower la flor
flute la flauta
following siguiente; **on**
  the following day al
  día siguiente
food la comida
foot el pie; **to go on**
  foot ir a pie
football el fútbol
for para, por
for example por ejemplo
for the rest por lo demás
forest el bosque
fortnight quince días

forward   adelante
fourth   cuarto, -a
free   libre
free time   el tiempo libre
French   francés, francesa
(on) Friday   el viérnes
friend   el amigo, la amiga
friendly   amable
from   de; desde
from . . . on   a partir de; desde
fruit   la fruta
funny   divertido, -a
furniture (*piece of*)   el mueble
future   el futuro

G

Galicia   Galicia
Galician   gallego
garage   el garaje
garden   el jardín
gate (*airport*)   la puerta
general: in general   en general
generally   generalmente, normalmente
gentle   suave
gentleman   el señor, el caballero
geography   la geografía
German   alemán, alemana
to get off   bajar de
to get on   subir a
to get up   levantarse
gift   el regalo
girl   la chica
to give   dar
to give (*as a present*)   regalar
give me!   ¡déme!
glass   el vaso
glasses (*spectacles*)   las gafas
to go   ir
to go abroad   ir al extranjero
to go away   irse
to go down   bajar
to go forward   avanzar
to go into   entrar (en)
to go on an excursion   ir de excursión
to go on foot   ir a pie
to go on holiday   ir de vacaciones
to go out   salir (de)
to go through   pasar por
to go to bed   acostarse /ue/
to go to mass   ir a misa
to go up   subir
good   bueno (buen), buena; (*of food*)   rico, -a
goodbye   adiós
good-looking   guapo, -a
goods lift   el montacargas
to govern   gobernar /ie/
government   el gobierno
government office   la oficina de Estado

grandfather   el abuelo
grandmother   la abuela
grant (*for study*)   la beca
grape   la uva
great   grande (gran)
green   verde
greeting   el saludo
ground   la tierra
ground-floor   la planta baja
group   el grupo
to grow   cultivar
to guess   adivinar
guide (*person*)   el guía
guidebook   la guía
guitar   la guitarra

H

hair   el pelo
hairdresser   el peluquero
hairdresser's   la peluquería
hake   la merluza
half   la mitad
half   medio, -a; half a year   medio año
hall   el vestíbulo
ham   el jamón
hand   la mano
handball   el balonmano
to happen   pasar
harbour   el puerto
to have (*own*)   tener
to have (*as auxiliary verb*)   haber
to have time   tener tiempo
to have been (ten years) in . . .   llevar (10 años) en . . .
he   él
head   la cabeza
head office   la oficina central
health   la salud
heap   el montón; heaps of   un montón de; muchos, -as
to heat   calentar /ie/
heart   el corazón
hello (*on phone*)   dígame
to help   ayudar
hen   la gallina
here   aquí
hereabouts   por aquí
to hide   esconder
high   alto, -a
to hire   alquilar
holy   santo, -a; sagrado, -a
holidays   las vacaciones; to go on holiday   ir de vacaciones
home   la casa; el hogar; at home   en casa
home town   el domicilio
homework   el deber, los deberes
hospital   el hospital
hot: it's hot   hace calor
hotel   el hotel; (*smaller*) el hostal

hour   la hora
house   la casa
how?   ¿cómo?
however   sin embargo
how many?   ¿cuántos? ¿cuántas?
how much?   ¿cuánto?
hug   el abrazo
hundred   ciento, cien
hunger   el hambre (*f*)
hungry: to be hungry   tener hambre
to hurt   doler /ue/; my leg hurts   me duele la pierna
husband   el marido

I

I   yo
I don't know   no sé (*saber*)
I like   me gusta (*gustar*)
I must   tengo que (*tener que*)
I myself   yo mismo
I think that   creo que . . .; me parece que . . .
identity card   el carnet de identidad
ice-cream   el helado
if   si
ill   malo, enfermo; to be ill   estar mal/malo, -a; enfermo
illiteracy   el analfabetismo
to imagine   imaginarse
immediately   en seguida
immigrant   el inmigrante
important   importante
imposing   impresionante
impression   la impresión
impressive   impresionante
in   en
in addition   además
in a short time   dentro de poco
in front of   delante (de)
in the evening   por la tarde
in the middle of   en el centro de
in the morning   por la mañana
in spite of   a pesar de
Inca   inca
including   incluso, hasta
Indian   el indio (*person*)
industry   la industria
influence   la influencia
ingredient   el ingrediente
inhabitant   el habitante
instruction   la instrucción
instrument   el instrumento
insulted   ofendido, -a
insurance company   la compañía de seguros
interesting   interesante
interview   la entrevista

interior   el interior
iron   el hierro
island   la isla
isn't it? *etc.*   ¿no?, ¿verdad?
Italian   el italiano (*person, language*)

J

jacket   la chaqueta; (*short, zip-up*) la cazadora
jeans   los vaqueros
jersey   el jersey
joke   la broma
journey   el viaje
juice   el jugo
jungle   la selva

K

key   la llave
kilo   el kilo
to kill   matar
kiosk   el quiosco (*also kiosko*)
kiss   el beso
kitchen   la cocina
knee   la rodilla
to know   (*a person or place*) conocer; (*a fact*) saber; I don't know   no sé

L

lady   la señora; young lady   la señorita
lake   el lago
lamp   la lámpara
land   la tierra (*soil*); el país (*country*)
landowner   el terrateniente
language   la lengua
large   grande (gran)
last (week)   (la semana) pasada
late   tarde; to be late   tardar; later on   más adelante
Latin America   América Latina, Latinoamérica
to learn   aprender
leather   el cuero
left   (*direction*) a la izquierda; to be left   quedar
leg   la pierna
lemon   el limón
less   menos; less than   menos que; (*with numbers*) menos de
lesson   la clase
letter   la carta
letter-box   el buzón
lettuce   la lechuga
life   la vida
lift   el ascensor
to light   encender /ie/
light-bulb   la bombilla
like   como

to **like** gustar; **I like to eat** me gusta comer
Lisbon Lisboa
to **listen (to)** escuchar
little pequeño, -a; **a little** un poco
to **live** vivir
living-room la sala de estar
long largo, -a
to **look at** mirar
to **look after** ocuparse de
to **look for** buscar
to **look like** parecer
lorry el camión
lot: a lot of, lots of un montón de; muchos, -as
loved querido, -a
low bajo, -a
luck la suerte
lunch el almuerzo; la comida

M

magazine la revista
to **make** hacer
male (chauvinist) pig el machista
man el señor, el hombre; **young man** el joven
manager el director
man(kind) el hombre
map el mapa; (*of a town*) el plano
market el mercado
married casado, -a
to **marry** casarse (con)
marvellous estupendo, -a
mass la misa; **to go to mass** ir a misa
material el material
mathematics las matemáticas
maybe quizás, a lo mejor
meadow el prado
meal la comida
medicine la medicina
meeting la cita
Mediterranean el Mediterráneo
melon el melón
Mexican mexicano, -a
Mexico City México D.F.
mild suave
military service el servicio militar; la mili
milk la leche
mine la mina
mineral water el agua mineral
Ministry el Ministerio
minus menos
misfortune la desgracia
modern moderno, -a
moment el momento; **just a moment!** ¡un momento!
(on) Monday el lunes
money el dinero
month el mes; **once a month, per month** al mes

monument el monumento
moon la luna
more más; **more than** más que; (*with numbers*) más de
moreover además
morning la mañana; **in the morning** por la mañana
most más
most of all sobre todo
mother la madre
Mother, Mum, Mummy mamá
Mr (el) señor; don
Mr and Mrs (los) señores
Mrs la mujer; (la) señora; doña
Miss (la) señorita
much mucho, -a
museum el museo
music la música
mussel el mejillón; la almeja
(one) must hay que
(I) must tengo que (*tener que*)

N

name el nombre
name-day el santo
narrow estrecho, -a
native indígena
naturally! ¡claro!
near cerca; **near to** cerca de
nearby cerca
nearly casi
neither ... nor ... ni ... ni ...
to **need** necesitar
negative negativo
nephew el sobrino
never (no ...) nunca
new nuevo, -a
newspaper el periódico
nice (*good-looking*) guapo, -a; bonito, -a; (*pleasant*) simpático, -a
niece la sobrina
night la noche; **at night** por la noche
no no
nobody, no-one (no ...) nadie; (no ...) ninguno, -a
north el norte
North American norteamericano, -a
not no
not until no ... hasta
not yet no ... todavía
nothing nada; (no ...) nada
now ahora; ya
nowadays hoy día
number el número

O

occasion la ocasión
occupation la profesión
to **occupy** ocupar
to **occupy (oneself) with** ocuparse de
of de
of course! ¡claro!
offended ofendido, -a
offer la oferta
office la oficina
office worker el/la oficinista
official oficial
official el empleado
often muchas veces
oil (*edible*) el aceite; (*petroleum*) el petroleo
O.K. muy bien, bueno
old viejo, -a;
older mayor;
oldest el/la mayor
olive la aceituna
olive tree el olivo
omelette la tortilla
on en, sobre
on the left/right of a la izquierda/derecha de
on the other hand por otro lado
on the outskirts of en las afueras de
on the shores of a orillas de
on Sunday el domingo (*etc.*)
once una vez; **at once** en seguida
onion la cebolla
only sólo; **the only** el único, la única
open abierto, -a
to **open** abrir
opinion: to give an opinion opinar
opposite enfrente
or o (*also* u, *see ¶ 89 E*)
orange la naranja
orchestra la orquesta
organization la organización
outskirts las afueras
oven el horno
over encima de; (= *more than*) más de (+ *number*)
overcoat el abrigo
to **owe** deber
own propio, -a
to **own** poseer
owner el dueño, la dueña

P

packet el paquete
page la página
painter el pintor
painting el cuadro
pair, a pair unos, unas; un par de
pamphlet el folleto
paprika (green/red pepper) el pimiento

parcel el paquete
parents los padres
to **park** (*a car*) aparcar
part la parte
to **pass** pasar
passing through de paso por
passport el pasaporte
passport office la gestoría
to **pay** pagar
peach el melocotón
pear la pera
peasant el campesino
peculiar raro, -a
pencil el lápiz
peninsula la península
people la gente
pepper (green/red) el pimiento
per cent por ciento
perfect perfecto, -a
perhaps quizás, a lo mejor
person la persona
petrol station la gasolinera
photograph la foto, la fotografía
piano el piano
picture (*drawing*) el dibujo; la imagen
picture (*painting*) el cuadro
picture postcard la postal
piece el trozo
pig el cerdo
pilot el piloto
place el sitio, el lugar
to **place** poner
plain la llanura
plane el avión
plate el plato
platform la plataforma
plastic el plástico
to **play** (*games*) jugar /ue/ a
to **play** (*instruments*) tocar
playing-card la carta
to **please** gustar; **pleased to meet you!** ¡mucho gusto!
pleasant agradable
politics la política
pollution la contaminación
poor pobre
poppy la amapola
population la población
porcelain la porcelana
porter (*caretaker*) el portero, la portera
porter's lodge la portería
positive positivo, -a
post-box (*number*) el apartado
postcard la postal
post-office la oficina de correos; **at the PO** en Correos
potato la patata

poverty la pobreza
practical práctico, -a
to practise practicar
prawn la gamba
precisely precisamente
preferably mejor
premises el local
to prepare preparar
present (estar) presente;
  at present actualmente
to present presentar
present (gift) el regalo
previous pasado, -a
price el precio; reduced
  price la rebaja; price
  list la lista de precios
primitive primitivo, -a
problem el problema
to produce producir
product el producto
production la
  producción
profession la profesión
property la propiedad
province la provincia
public el público
pullover el jersey
pupil el alumno, la
  alumna
purchase la compra
pure puro, -a
to put poner
to put on ponerse
pyramid la pirámide

Q

quality la calidad
quarter (district) el barrio
quarter (of an hour) el
  cuarto (de hora)
question pregunta
quick, quickly rápido
quite bastante; quite a
  lot bastante

R

radio la radio
rain la lluvia
to rain llover /ue/; it's
  raining llueve
rapid rápido
to read leer
real real
to realize (carry
  out) realizar
really realmente
to receive recibir
receptionist el/la
  recepcionista
record el disco
record-player el
  tocadiscos
red rojo, -a
refrigerator el
  frigorífico
region la región
registration plate la
  matrícula
relation, relative el
  pariente

to remain quedar
to remember acordarse
  /ue/
to rent alquilar
to reply contestar
to reserve reservar
to rest descansar
restaurant el restaurante
to return regresar, volver
  /ue/
rice el arroz
rich rico, -a
right (direction) a la
  derecha
ring el anillo
to ring (bell or
  telephone) sonar /ue/
to ring someone
  up llamar a alguien
  (por teléfono)
ripe maduro, -a
river el río
road el camino; (main
  road) la carretera
Roman romano, -a
room la habitación, el
  cuarto
rug la alfombra
to rule gobernar /ie/
to run correr

S

sacred sagrado, -a;
  santo, -a
sale la venta; (clearance)
  la liquidación
salesman el vendedor
sales manager el jefe de
  ventas
sale price la rebaja
same (el) mismo, (la)
  misma
sandwich el bocadillo
sardine la sardina
sausage el salchichón
satisfied satisfecho, -a;
  contento, -a
(on) Saturday el sábado
to say decir
scene la escena
scholarship (grant) la
  beca
science la ciencia
school la escuela
  (primary); el instituto
  (State); el colegio
  (private)
schoolday el día de clase
sculpture la escultura
sea el mar
second segundo, -a
to see ver; let's see! ¡a
  ver!
to seek buscar
to seem parecer; it
  seems that parece que
to sell vender
to send enviar
sensational sensacional
sentence la frase
serious grave
several varios, -as

to shave afeitarse
she ella
shellfish el marisco
shirt la camisa
to shock chocar
shoe el zapato; sports
  shoes las zapatillas
  deportivas
shop la tienda
to shop comprar
shop window el
  escaparate
short corto, -a; (of height)
  bajo, -a
to show mostrar /ue/
shower la ducha
to shower ducharse
shut cerrado, -a
to shut cerrar /ie/
side el lado; at the side
  of al lado de
sideburns las patillas
to sign firmar
signal la señal
signature la firma
since (because) porque;
  como; (time) desde;
  since 19.. desde 19..
single room la
  (habitación) individual
sister la hermana
situated (estar) situado,
  -a
six months medio año
the Sixties los años 60
size (clothes) la talla
to skate patinar
to ski esquiar
ski-slope la pista
skirt la falda
sky el cielo
to sleep dormir /ue/
slim delgado, -a
small pequeño, -a; (of
  height) bajo, -a
smell (of) el olor (a)
smoke el humo
to smoke fumar
to snow nevar /ie/; it's
  snowing nieva
so tan
so, so it is así
so, in other words ¡eh!
  pues
social social
social sciences las
  ciencias sociales
sock el calcetín
sofa el sofá
soft drink el refresco
some unos, unas; un par
  de; algunos, -as
someone alguien;
  alguno (algún), alguna
something algo
son el hijo
song la canción
soon pronto; dentro de
  poco
sorry perdón, lo siento
soup la sopa
south el sur
south-east el sureste

sowing-machine la
  sembradora
Spain España; el Estado
  español
Spaniard el español, la
  española
Spanish español, -a
Spanish (language) el
  español; el castellano
Spanish-America
  Hispanoamérica
to speak hablar; is
  spoken se habla
special especial
spectacles las gafas
to spend (time) pasar;
  (money) gastar
sport el deporte
sports shoes las
  zapatillas deportivas
spring la primavera
squid el calamar
stairs la escalera
stamp el sello
to stand (location) estar;
  encontrarse /ue/
state el estado
station la estación
stationer's la papelería
to stay quedar; quedarse
to steal robar
still todavía
stomach el estómago
store los almacenes
strange raro, -a
straw la paja
strawberry la fresa
street la calle
stroll el paseo
strong fuerte
struggle la lucha
student el estudiante
to study estudiar
study-visit la visita de
  estudios
style el estilo
suit el traje
suitcase la maleta
summer el verano
(on) Sunday el domingo
sun el sol; it's
  sunny hace sol
supermarket el
  supermercado, el super
sure seguro, -a; cierto, -a
surname el apellido
surroundings los
  alrededores
sweet (taste) dulce
to swim nadar
swimming-pool la
  piscina

T

table la mesa
tall alto, -a
to talk hablar
to take tomar
to take a bath bañarse
to take a shower
  ducharse
to take time tardar

to **take a walk/stroll** ir de paseo, dar una vuelta
to **take out** sacar
tape la cinta
task la tarea
taste el gusto
taxi el taxi
taxi-driver el/la taxista
tea el té
teacher el profesor, la profesora
team el equipo
tee-shirt el niki
telephone el teléfono
telephone kiosk la cabina
telephone receiver el auricular
telephone conversation la llamada (telefónica)
television la televisión, la tele
television set el televisor
to **tell** (*a story*) contar /ue/
temperature la temperatura
tennis el tenis
tension la tensión
terrace la terraza
text el texto
thank you very much muchas gracias
thanks (for) gracias (por)
thanks to gracias a
that (*which, who*) que
that aquel, aquella; **that one** aquél; aquélla
theatre el teatro
then (*at that time*) entonces
then (*next*) luego
there allí, ahí
there is, there are hay
therefore porque
these estos, estas
they ellos, ellas
thief el ladrón
thing la cosa
to **think** pensar /ie/; creer
third tercero (tercer), -a
thirst la sed; **to be thirsty** tener sed
this este, esta
this one éste, ésta
those aquellos, aquellas
through por
(on) Thursday el jueves
thus así
ticket el billete
tie la corbata
tights los pantys
time el tiempo; (*occasion*) la vez

timetable el horario
tired cansado, -a
to a; hasta
tobacco el tabaco
today hoy
together juntos, -as; **all together** en total
toilets los servicios
tomato el tomate
tomorrow mañana; **tomorrow morning** mañana por la mañana; **the day after tomorrow** pasado mañana
ton la tonelada
tone (*dialling*) la señal
too, too much demasiado
to **touch** tocar
tourism el turismo
tourist el/la turista
towards hacia
town la cuidad
tractor el tractor
traditional tradicional
traffic el tráfico
tragedy la tragedia; **what a tragedy!** ¡qué tragedia!
to **train** entrenar
transistor radio el transistor
to **transport** transportar
to **travel** viajar
travel agency la agencia de viajes
tree el árbol
trousers el pantalón
truck el camión
trumpet la trompeta
truth la verdad
to **try on** probar /ue/, probarse /ue/
(on) Tuesday el martes
twice as much el doble
two dos; **in twos** de dos en dos

U

ugh! ¡uf!
uncle el tío
under debajo de
underground (railway) el metro
to **underline** subrayar
to **understand** entender /ie/
undoubtedly sin duda
unemployed (estar) en paro
university la universidad
unknown desconocido
to **unload** descargar
unmarried soltero, -a

unmarried woman la soltera
unmarried man el soltero
unripe verde
until hasta
up arriba
USA los Estados Unidos, los EE.UU.
to **use** utilizar
usually generalmente, normalmente

V

value el valor
vanilla la vainilla
various varios, -as
vegetable la hortaliza
very muy; mucho (*see ¶ 13*)
via por
village el pueblo; el poblado; (*small*) el pueblecito
violent violento, -a
visit la visita
to **visit** visitar
vocabulary el vocabulario
volley-ball el volibol

W

waistcoat el chaleco
to **wait (for)** esperar
waiter el camarero
waitress la camarera
walk el paseo
to **want** querer /ie/
war la guerra
to **wash** lavar
watch el reloj
to **watch** mirar
water el agua (*f*)
water-melon la sandía
way la forma
we nosotros, -as
wealth la riqueza
to **wear** (*clothes*) llevar
weather el tiempo; **the weather's bad** hace mal tiempo; **the weather's fine** hace buen tiempo
week la semana; **next week** la semana que viene
weekend el fin de semana
weekdays (los) días laborables
well bien; **to be well** estar bien
west el oeste
what? ¿qué?; **what is the time** ¿qué hora es?;

what do you think? ¿qué te parece?
wheat el trigo
when cuando
when? ¿cuándo?
where donde
where? ¿dónde?
where to? ¿adónde?
which que
which? ¿qué?, ¿cuál?, ¿cuáles?
while mientras
white blanco, -a
who que, quien
who? ¿quién?
whole todo, -a; entero, -a; **the whole world** todo el mundo, el mundo entero
whose? ¿de quién?
why? ¿por qué?
widespread extenso, -a
wife la mujer
wind el viento; **it's windy** hace viento
windmill el molino de viento
window la ventana
wine el vino
winter el invierno
to **wish** desear
with con
without sin; **without doubt** sin duda
woman la mujer; **young woman** la joven
wood (*forest*) el bosque
wool la lana
work el trabajo
work of art la obra
to **work** trabajar
to **work as** trabajar de
worker el trabajador
working hours el horario
world el mundo
wrapped envuelto, -a
to **write** escribir

Y

year el año; **a year, per year** al año
yellow amarillo
yet todavía
yes sí
yesterday ayer
you (*informal*) tú (*sing*); vosotros, vosotras (*pl*)
you (*formal*) usted (*sing*), ustedes (*pl*)
young joven
young man el joven
young woman la joven
younger menor
youngest el/la menor

promoting any 'label' simply because it is new and therefore untainted. Moreover, the energy invested in the promotions exercise may dissipate the enthusiasm needed to promote unity. Nor would I want the reader to be distracted by such a mischievous invention, particularly if the more serious points of this study were overlooked. Finally, it has to be admitted that the term is somewhat arbitrary. Since there are an abundance of terms already being proposed, I could see no reason why I too should not indulge myself. Besides, the term 'lappilli' is as good as any and better than others, although it may be a little while before the term finds its way into everyday usage or the pages of the *Sunday Times*.

Prospects for the future

At the time of writing, two of the more obvious questions regarding the future are whether the Conservatives will soon be winkled out of power and, if they are, what difference will it make? If the Labour Party were to be elected, there would almost definitely be a wave of disputes because workers would hope to restore parity with other groups, restore differentials and exert control over working practices. Despite the decline in membership in the 1980s, trade unionism is deeply embedded in British culture. Any review of trade union history would show that during periods of upswing in the economy, or when political conditions are favourable, people look to a trade union to improve their living standards. If the leadership failed to lead, then the shop stewards' movement would get a new lease of life. In either case, it would be all too easy to degenerate into the kind of sectionalism of the past. Moreover, a shift in the balance of power *between* classes need not reduce divisions *within* the working class. As Parkin shows it is possible for groups to be more exclusive towards members of their own class if they are attempting to challenge the dominant class. The affect of dual closure may enable well-placed workers to improve wages, consumption patterns and occupational welfare benefits, but will do little for the poor. Without massive injections of cash for training and rigorously policed affirmative action policies, it is difficult to imagine single parents, the long-term unemployed or disaffected black youth being offered jobs in the most lucrative trades and industries.

Alternatively, it may be that organized labour will try and represent a broader constituency. This rather more optimistic scenario could point to efforts made by some unions to recruit part-timers and short-term contract staff. The TUC's support for equal opportunities and sustained criticism of racial discrimination might add weight to this view. There have already been some serious attempts at extending occupational welfare to part-time workers (Mann and Anstee, 1989). A return to the low levels of unemployment associated with the 1950s and 1960s would be a fairly major achievement in the next few years but, again, not one which would necessarily assist the poor. Trade unionists would be inclined to ask for additional perks and these might be extended to some groups of low-paid workers. At the same time skilled workers would be likely to ask for further improvements, and with the possibility of labour shortages employers might be inclined to offer such benefits. In such circumstances, the more locally orientated negotiations associated with the 1980s would encourage regional variations in pay and income. Geographical divides could widen and government would be asked to 'interfere' in the market, something Labour has said it is reluctant to do.

When organized labour has mounted a more coherent challenge to capital, it has done so through reformist social democratic channels. Despite the language of universalism and the existence of a coherent section of the labour movement pressing for socialist policies, the specific interests of women and ethnic groups are pushed aside. Social democracy is not simply the shell within which corporatism develops (Jessop, 1979), but also the golden egg which the poor are prevented from sharing. Thus a dynamic working class may improve public welfare provision but specific social groups will still be relatively poorer within it.

Policies that might reduce intra-class divisions would require the organized labour movement to sacrifice some of its power, something trade unionists and Labour Party leaders are reluctant to do. If organizations of the poor – not the pressure groups for the poor – were given a political voice, change might be possible. The reason for wanting the poor to be involved in the political process is that they can see more clearly than anyone the obstacles they confront. Whether the Labour Party, trade unions and trade councils would let claimants, black organizations, and single parents affiliate as separately organized groups is doubtful. It would require a measure of bravery on the part of the current labour movement leadership which seems to be absent. If any attempts were bolstered by a transformative vision for the twenty-first century, there would be the possibility of reducing social divisions. However, it is difficult to be optimistic.

The most likely scenario is that the political constituency for maintaining the SDW in its present form will ensure that any truly redistributive policies will be suppressed. Currently, public debate on the poor seems to be moving closer to seeing them as some sort of underclass, with all the implications this has for authoritarian and selective social policies. With middle-class observers focusing on lone parents, the long-term unemployed, street crime and the homeless, the possibility of public welfare being 'reserved for the poor' is increasingly likely. Mortgage interest rates, a buoyant labour market, a good pension, holidays and enjoying the benefits of access to fiscal and occupational welfare, are the concerns of the bulk of the working class. Improvements in the provision of public welfare, with possibly the exception of the NHS and education which have a large middle-class clientele, are unlikely in the face of such a strong demand from a larger constituency for occupational and fiscal welfare. Nor am I condemning such pragmatic concerns when the alternative is so uncertain and the trench of dependency threatens every member of the working class. If I were still an AEUW convenor, I would be looking forward to the return of a Labour government, not because it would transform society, but because I would be able to press for a general improvement in my members' position, which is the prime objective of trade unionism.

If Labour fails to gain office, the prospect is even more bleak. The pattern of intra-class divisions discussed in Chapter 5 will be reinforced. The possibility of unemployment benefit being abolished in favour of some sort of 'workfare' is very real. Changes in education and health policy (for example, Opting Out and Local Management of Schools) are likely to mean that 'The Growing Divide' (Walker and Walker, 1987) will be a yawning chasm by the end of the century. Labour may do little to end intra-class divisions, but the Conservatives will surely make them concrete. In order to remain in office, the Conservatives have to appeal to sections of the working class. The Conservative Party needs only to identify those relatively well-placed sections of the working class and persuade them that Labour might cut their fiscal benefits (e.g. mortgage income tax relief) or increase their tax burden by increasing public welfare, to improve their electoral chances. Alternatively, if they can improve on the current occupational welfare package by extending tax allowances, they may stay in power and widen the SDW.

Putting aside my crystal ball, it is clear that the SDW will continue to reflect changes in the production and consumption processes. Simultaneously, and as argued at various points the SDW both reinforces social divisions and promotes further fractures. In particular, the SDW makes it extremely difficult to construct political alliances over social policy issues. The Friendly Societies in the nineteenty century, the national insurance schemes in the first half of the twentieth century and occupational and fiscal welfare today, encourage the marginalization of the poor.

Divided by welfare?

This book began by highlighting the dangers of terms like 'the underclass'. There is throughout a genuine concern that the observations, or discourse as Foucault's supporters might prefer to call it, of the poor construct a particular knowledge base. These observations can then serve to reinforce the powerful and disaggregate the powerless. Sinfield (1978, p.149) was entirely correct to consider power an under-theorized element of the SDW in which the 'visibility' of public welfare makes the poor more vulnerable to exposure and punitive measures. In this context, Cook's (1989) work on the different responses to tax and benefit fraud exposes the privileges of the powerful and the punishment of the weak.

Titmuss was wrong to tie 'man-made' dependencies to industrialization, and it is alienation, rather than anomie, which is promoted by capitalism and the labour process. This point has been heavily qualified, however, and the impact of specific pre-capitalist social divisions has been emphasized throughout. The competition generated by capitalism, combined with the individuating effects of the labour process, both encourage sectionalism and increase the vulnerability of sections of the working class. It is in response to dependency that the working class 'makes' the SDW through the form and direction of class struggle.

It has been shown in Chapters 3–5 that historically the working class has formed defence organizations that were exclusive. Exclusion, or 'closure' as Parkin (1979) calls it, was based on a combination of actuarial principles, xenophobia and patriarchal logic. We have also discussed the manner in which sections of the working class combine in order to protect themselves from the worst effects of capitalist social relations. Those groups with some leverage over the labour process have been able to exert this and improve their position in the labour market. The fluidity and contested nature of the labour process ensure that different sections of the working class are able to exert leverage at different moments. There are, however, some groups who are constantly excluded.

Racism and patriarchy have been recurring themes in the promotion of intra-class divisions, even if skill has been a more fluid concept. Changes in technology and the labour process, the composition of available labour, and the overall balance of forces between capital and labour, have all affected the ability of different sections of the working class to establish a measure of security within an insecure economic system. The reassertion of market principles that has taken place in the 1980s has, as we saw in Chapter 5, encouraged both workers and management to pursue their needs through the occupational and fiscal systems of welfare. Or, rather more often, to obtain occupational welfare benefits which are also underpinned by fiscal policy.

The stark reality is that those who can gain access to occupational and fiscal welfare almost invariably receive more benefits and a better service. Quite sensibly, socialists have not refused to join pension schemes or profit-sharing arrangements, accept transport allowances, take cheap mortgages, and so on. The only significant 'benefit' that has been rejected on principle has been private health insurance. Indeed, it is because occupational and fiscal welfare benefits and services are 'better' that they are socially divisive. If the occupational and fiscal welfare systems were simply different, rather than being inequitable, we might applaud the choice and variation they provided. Supporters of a 'mixed economy of welfare', or 'welfare plural-ism', fail to acknowledge that it is because occupational and fiscal welfare systems are more attractive that they exist (Beresford and Croft, 1984; Bosanquet, 1984; Donnison, 1984). If there really were equity between the different systems of welfare, there would be little point, for the beneficiaries, in pursuing occupational and fiscal welfare.

The development of occupational and fiscal welfare has not benefited the poor. The most notable feature in the changing landscape of welfare provi-sion in recent years has been the growth in social divisions which are rein-forced by the SDW. Part-time workers, the unemployed, single parents, the irregularly employed, the elderly, the physically handicapped and the low paid are still essentially dependent upon public welfare. They have to rely upon the most visible and stigmatized benefits which provide the least security. Public welfare also often serves to reinforce exclusion from the patterns of consumption that accompany occupational and fiscal welfare. Despite the changes that have occurred since Titmuss wrote his original essay on the SDW, it remains the case that for all those who have no alternative but to turn to public welfare when they are in need, the fall into the trench of dependency is more likely, and the climb out of it more difficult.

The struggle to be the well-placed workers of tomorrow is always taking place today. It is significant that the services and benefits that trade unions offer are seen by some commentators as an important aspect of the inter-union jostling for position (Bassett, 1986; Leadbeater, 1987). If the unions and staff associations representing white-collar and supervisory staff press for occupational welfare – cheap mortgages, low interest loans, travel and car allowances and a host of other 'fringes' – the manual unions who are able to do so will follow suit. Similarly, there is already widespread support for fiscal welfare, e.g. tax relief on mortgages, which will make it hard for any government radically to alter current fiscal policy in favour of the poor. As the number of people who rely on public welfare declines, so too will the political constituency for improvements in it. As the gap widens between those who have access to fiscal and occupational welfare and those who have to rely on public welfare, there is a temptation for middle–class observers to identify an 'underclass'. It is a temptation which has to be resisted if the process of 'making' an underclass is not to be built into new state policies. Otherwise, the impact on intra-class divisions and the SDW could well be to recreate the sort of distinctions, between those at the top and those at the bottom of the working class, which existed in Victorian Britain.

Bibliography

Abercrombie, N., Hill, S. and Turner, B. (1980). *The Dominant Ideology Thesis.* George Allen and Unwin, London.

Addison, P. (1975). *The Road to 1945.* Cape, London.

Aglietta, M. (1987). *A Theory of Capitalist Regulation: The U.S. Experience.* Verso, London.

Alcock, P. (1987). *Poverty and State Support.* Longman, London.

Alexander, S. (1976). Women's work in nineteenth century London: A study of the years 1820–1850. In Mitchell, J. and Oakley, A. (eds), *The Rights and Wrongs of Women.* Penguin, Harmondsworth.

Althusser, L. (1969). *For Marx.* Penguin, Harmondsworth.

Anderson, P. (1980). *Arguments Within English Marxism.* Verso, London.

Andrzejewski, S. L. (1954). *Military Organisation and Society.* Routledge and Kegan Paul, London.

Anthias, F. (1980). Women and the Reserve Army of Labour: A critique of Veronica Beechey. *Capital and Class*, 10: 50–63.

Armstrong, P. (1988). Labour and monopoly capital. In Hyman, R. and Streek, W. (eds), *New Technology and Industrial Relations.* Basil Blackwell, Oxford.

Arnott, H. (1987). Second class citizens. In Walker, A. and Walker, C. (eds), *The Growing Divide: A Social Audit 1979–87.* CPAG, London.

Ashworth, M. and Dilnot, A. (1987). Company cars taxation. *Fiscal Studies*, 8 (4): 24–38.

Atkinson, J. (1984). Manpower strategies for flexible organisations. *Personnel Management*, August, 18–21.

Atkinson, J. and Gregory, D. (1986). A flexible future. *Marxism Today*, April, 12–17.

Audit Commission (1986). *Managing the Crisis in Council Housing.* HMSO, London.

Bagguley, P. (1989). *The Post-Fordist Enigma: Theories of Labour Flexibility.* Lancaster Regionalism Group, Working Paper No. 29, February.

Bagguley, P. (1991). *From Protest to Aquiescence: Political Movements of the Unemployed.* Macmillan, London.

Barbalet, J.M. (1982). Social closure in class analysis: A critique of Parkin. *Sociology*, 16 (4): 484–97.

Barnett, C. (1986). *The Audit of War; The Illusion and Reality of Britain as a Great Nation.* Macmillan, London.

Barrett, M. (1980). *Women's Oppression Today: Some Problems in Marxist Feminist Analysis*. New Left Books, London.

Barron, R.D. and Norris, G.M. (1976). Sexual divisions and the dual labour market. In Barker, D.L. and Allen, S. (eds), *Dependence and Exploitation in Work and Marriage*. Longman, London.

Bassett, P. (1986). *Strike Free: New Industrial Relations in Britain*. Macmillan, London.

Beechey, V. (1978). Women and production: A critical analysis of some sociological theories of women's work. In Kuhn, A. and Wolpe, A. (eds), *Feminism and Materialism: Women and Modes of Production*. Routledge and Kegan Paul, London.

Belchem, J. (1985). English working class radicalism and the Irish, 1815–1850. In Swift, I. and Gilley, R. (eds), *The Irish in the Victorian City*. Croom Helm, London.

Beresford, P. and Croft, S. (1984). Welfare pluralism: The new face of Fabianism. *Critical Social Policy*, 9: 19–39.

Best, G.F.A. (1972). *Mid-Victorian Britain 1851–1875*. Shoken, New York.

Beynon, H. (1973). *Working for Ford*. Penguin, Harmondsworth.

Black, D. (1980). *Inequalities in Health*. Report of a Research Working Party chaired by Sir Douglas Black. DHSS, London.

Blackburn, R. and Mann, M. (1979). *The Working Class and the Labour Market*. Macmillan, London.

Blackburn, R. and Mann, M. (1981). The dual labour market model. In Braham, P., Rhodes, E. and Pearn, M. (eds), *Discrimination and Disadvantage in Employment: The Experience of Black Workers*. Harper and Row/Open University Press, London/Milton Keynes.

Booth, A. (1989). *Raising the Roof on Housing Myths*. Shelter, London.

Bosanquet, N. (1984). Is privatisation inevitable. In Le Grand, J. and Robinson, R. (eds), *Privatisation and the Welfare State*. George Allen and Unwin, London.

Boston, S. (1980). *Women Workers and the Trade Union Movement*. Davis-Poynter, London.

Bovenkerk, F. (1984). The rehabilitation of the rabble: How and why Marx and Engels wrongly depicted the lumpen-proletariat as a reactionary force. *The Netherlands Journal of Sociology (Sociologicia Neerlandica)*, 20 (1): 13–42.

Bowles, S. and Gintis, H. (1976). *Schooling in Capitalist America*. Basic Books, New York.

Bradley, H. (1986). Change and the development of gender-based job segregation in the labour process. In Knights, D. and Wilmott, H. (eds), *Gender and the Labour Process*. Gower, Aldershot.

Braverman, H. (1974). *Labor and Monopoly Capital*. Monthly Review Press, New York.

Braybon, G. (1981). *Women Workers in the First World War: The British Experience*. Croom Helm, London.

Braybon, G. and Summerfield, P. (1987). *Out of the Cage: Women's Experiences in Two World Wars*. Pandora/Routledge and Kegan Paul, London.

Briggs, E. and Deacon, A. (1973). The creation of the Unemployment Assistance Board. *Policy and Politics*, 2 (1): 43–62.

Brown, G. (1977). *Sabotage*. Spokesman Books, Nottingham.

Building Societies Association (1989). *Housing and Saving*. BSA, London.

Burgess, K. (1980). *The Challenge of Labour*. Croom Helm, London.

Buswell, C. (1987). Training for low pay. In Glendinning, C. and Millar, J. (eds), *Women and Poverty in Britain*. Wheatsheaf, Brighton.

Byrne, D. and Parson, D. (1983). The state and the reserve army: The management of class relations in space. In Anderson, J., Duncan S. and Hudson, R. (eds), *Redundant Spaces in Cities and Regions: Studies in Industrial Decline and Social Change*. Institute of British Geographers Special Publication No.15. Academic Press, London.

Campling, J. (1990). Social policy digest. *Journal of Social Policy*, **19** (1): 93–112.

Castells, M. (1978). *City, Class and Power*. Macmillan, London

Castles, F.G. (1985). *The Working Class and Welfare*. George Allen and Unwin, London.

Castles, S. and Kosack, G. (1972). The function of labour immigration in Western European capitalism. *New Left Review*, **73**: 3–21.

Castles, S. and Kosack, G. (1973). *Immigrant Workers and Class Structure in Western Europe*. Oxford University Press, Oxford.

Charles, L. and Duffin, L. (eds) (1985). *Women and Work in Pre-Industrial England*. Croom Helm, London.

Clark, J. (1988). *The Process of Technological Change: New Technology and Social Choice in the Work Place*. Cambridge University Press, Cambridge.

Clarke, S. (1977). Marxism, sociology and Poultanzas' theory of the state. *Capital and Class*, Summer, 1–31.

Coates, K. and Topham, T. (1986). *Trade Unions and Politics*. Basil Blackwell, Oxford.

Cockburn, C. (1983). *Brothers: Male Dominance and Technological Change*. Pluto Press, London.

Cohen, S. (1985). Anti-Semitism, immigration controls and the welfare state. *Critical Social Policy*, **13**: 73–92.

Cole, G.D.H. and Postgate, R. (1961). *The British Common People 1746–1946*. Methuen, London.

Cook, D. (1989). *Rich Law, Poor Law: Different Responses to Tax and Supplementary Benefit Fraud*. Open University Press, Milton Keynes.

Corrigan, P. and Leonard, P. (1978). *Social Work Practice Under Capitalism: A Marxist Approach*. Macmillan, London

Cousins, C. (1987). *Controlling Social Welfare: A Sociology of State Welfare, Work and Organisation*. Wheatsheaf, Brighton.

Crompton, R. and Jones, G. (1984). *White Collar Proletariat: Deskilling and Gender in Clerical Work*. Macmillan, London.

Cronin, J.E. (1979). *Industrial Conflict in Modern Britain*. Croom Helm, London.

Cronin, J.E. (1984). *Labour and Society in Britain 1918–1979*, Batsford, London.

Crossick, G. (1978). *An Artisan Elite in Victorian Society*. Croom Helm, London.

Crouch, C. (1979). *The Politics of Industrial Relations*. Fontana/Collins, Glasgow.

Crouch, C. (1982). *The Logic of Collective Action*. Collins, Glasgow.

Crowther, M.A. (1978). The later years of the workhouse 1890–1929. In Thane, P. (ed.), *The Origins of British Social Policy*. London, Croom Helm.

Crowther, M.A. (1981). *The Workhouse System 1834–1929: The History of an English Social Institution*. Batsford, London.

Dahrendorf, R. (1988). *The Modern Social Conflict*. Weidenfeld and Nicholson, London.

Deacon, A. (1976). *In Search of the Scrounger: The Administration of Unemployment Insurance in Britain 1920–31*. Occasional Papers in Social Administration, No. 60. Social Administration Research Trust, London.

Deacon, A. (1977). Concession and coercion: The politics of unemployment insurance in the twenties. In Briggs, A. and Saville, J. (eds), *Essays in Labour History*, Vol. 3. Croom Helm, London.

Deacon, A. (1981). Unemployment and politics since 1945. In Showler, B. and Sinfield, A. (eds), *The Workless State*. Martin Robertson, Oxford.

Deacon, A. (1984). Was there a consensus? Social policy in the 1940s. In Jones, C. and Stevenson, J. (eds), *Yearbook of Social Policy in Britain 1983*. Routledge and Kegan Paul, London.

Deacon, A. and Bradshaw, J. (1983). *Reserved for the Poor*. Basil Blackwell, Oxford.

Doeringer, P. and Piore, M. J. (1971). *Internal Labour Markets and Manpower Analysis*. Heath, Lexington, Mass.

Donnison,. D. (1979). Social policy since Titmuss. *Journal of Social Policy*, **8** (2): 145–57.

Donnison, D. (1982). *The Politics of Poverty*. Martin Robertson, Oxford.

Donnison, D. (1984). The progressive potential of privatisation. In Le Grand, J. and Robinson, R. (eds), *Privatisation and the Welfare State*. George Allen and Unwin, London.

Dow, J.C.R. (1964). *The Management of the British Economy 1945–1960*. Cambridge University Press, Cambridge.

Drake, B. (1984). *Women in Trade Unions*. Virago Press, London.

Dunleavy, P. (1980). *Urban Political Analysis*. Macmillan, London.

Dunleavy, P. (1986). Sectoral cleavages and the stabilization of state expenditures. *Environment and Planning: Society and Space*, **4**: 128–44.

Durkheim, E. (1933). *The Division of Labour in Society*. Free Press, New York.

Edwards, R. (1979). *Contested Terrain: The Transformation of Work in the Twentieth Century*. Heinemann, London.

Elster, J. (1985). *Making Sense of Marx*. Cambridge University Press, Cambridge.

Elster, J. (1986). *Karl Marx: A Reader*. Cambridge University Press, Cambridge.

Engels, F. (1958). *The Condition of the Working Class in England*. Basil Blackwell, Oxford.

EOC (1985). *Model of Equality*. A consulting actuary's report on the methods and costs of equalising the treatment of men and women in occupational pension schemes. Prepared by Duncan C. Fraser and Co. for the Equal Opportunities Commission.

Esping-Andersen, G. (1990). *The Three Worlds of Welfare Capitalism*. Polity, Cambridge.

Field, F. (1981). *Inequality in Britain*. Fontana, Glasgow.

Field, F. (1989). *Losing Out: The Emergence of Britain's Underclass*. Basil Blackwell, Oxford.

Field, F. (1990). Britain's underclass. In Murray, C., *The Emerging British UNDERCLASS*. IEA Health and Welfare Unit, London.

Fitzgerald, R. (1988). *British Labour Management and Industrial Welfare 1846–1939*. Croom Helm, London.

Flynn, R. (1988). Political aquiescence, privatisation and residualisation in British housing policy. *Journal of Social Policy*, **17** (3): 289–312.

Forrest, R. and Murie, A. (1983). Residualisation and council housing: Aspects of the changing social relations of housing tenure. *Journal of Social Policy*, **12** (4): 453–68.

Forrest, R. and Murie, A. (1986). Marginalization and subsidized individualism: The sale of council houses in the restructuring of the British Welfare State. *International Journal of Urban and Regional Research*, **10** (1): 46–66.

Forrest, M. and Murie, A. (1989). Fiscal reorientation, centralization and the privatization of council housing. In McDowell, L., Sarre, P. and Hamnett, C. (eds),

Divided Nation: Social and Cultural Change in Britain. Hodder and Stoughton, London.

Foster, J. (1974). *Class Struggle and the Industrial Revolution.* Methuen, London.

Fox, A. (1985). *Man Mismanagement.* Hutchinson, London.

Fraser, D. (1984). *The Evolution of the British Welfare State.* Macmillan, London.

Friend, A. and Metcalf, A. (1981). *Slump City.* Pluto Press, London.

Fry, V.C., Hammond, E.M. and Kay, J.A. (1985). *Taxing Pensions: The Taxation of Occupational Pension Schemes in the U.K.* Institute of Fiscal Studies, London.

Fryer, P. (1984). *Staying Power: The History of Black People in Britain.* Pluto Press, London.

Galbraith, J.K. (1967). *The New Industrial State.* Penguin, Harmondsworth.

Gamble, A. (1974). *The Conservative Nation.* Routledge and Kegan Paul, London.

Gamble, A. (1985). *Britain in Decline: Economic Policy, Political Strategy and the British State.* Macmillan, London.

Giddens, A. (1973). *The Class Structure of the Advanced Societies.* Hutchinson, London.

Giddens, A. (1978). *Durkheim.* Fontana/Collins, Glasgow.

Giddens, A. (1980). Classes, capitalism and the state. *Theory and Society,* 9: 877–90.

Ginsburg, N. (1979). *Class Capital and Social Policy.* Macmillan, London.

Glendinning, C. and Millar, J. (eds) (1987). *Women and Poverty in Britain.* Wheatsheaf, Brighton.

Glyn, A. and Harrison, J. (1980). *The British Economic Disaster.* Pluto Press, London.

Golding, P. (ed.) (1986). *Excluding the Poor.* CPAG, London.

Golding, P. and Middleton, S. (1982). *Images of Welfare.* Martin Robertson, Oxford.

Goldthorpe, D., Lockwood, J., Bechhoffer, F. and Platt, J. (1968). *The Affluent Worker: Industrial Attitudes and Behaviour.* Cambridge University Press, Cambridge.

Goodin, R.E. and Le Grand, J., with Dryzek, J., Gibson, D.M., Hanson, R.L., Haveman, R.H. and Winter, D. (1987). *Not Only the Poor: The Middle Classes and the Welfare State.* Allen and Unwin, London

Gosden, P.H.J.H. (1961). *The Friendly Societies in England, 1815–1875.* Manchester University Press, Manchester.

Gosden, P.H.J.H. (1973). *Self-help Voluntary Associations in the 19th Century.* Batsford, London

Gough, I. (1979). *The Political Economy of the Welfare State.* Macmillan, London.

Government Actuary Report (1983). *Seventh Survey.* HMSO, London.

Gray, R. (1976). *The Labour Aristocracy in Victorian Edinburgh.* Oxford University Press. Oxford.

Green, F., Hadjimatheou, G. and Smail, R. (1984). *Unequal Fringes: Fringe Benefits in the United Kingdom.* Low Pay Unit, London.

Gregg, P. (1976). *Black Death to Industrial Revolution: A Social and Economic History of England.* Harrap, London

Groves, D. (1987). Occupational pension provision and women's poverty in old age. In Glendinning, C. and Millar, J. (eds), *Women and Poverty in Britain.* Wheatsheaf, Brighton.

Halevy, E. (1961). *History of the English People in the Nineteenth Century,* Vols 5 and 6. Benn, London.

Hall, S. and Schwarz, B. (1985). State and society 1880–1930. In Langan, M. and Schwarz, B. (eds), *Crises in the British State 1880–1930.* Hutchinson, London.

Halsey, A.H. (1989). Social trends since World War II. In McDowell, L., Sarre, P. and Hamnett, C. (eds), *Divided Nation: Social and Cultural Change in Britain.* Hodder and Stoughton, London.

Hannah, L. (1986). *Inventing Retirement: The Development of Occupational Pensions in Britain.* Cambridge University Press, Cambridge.

Hannington, W. (1973). *Unemployed Struggles 1919–1936.* E.P. Publishing, East Ardsley.

Hansard (1908). Vol. 190, 4th Series, June 1908, Cols 565–566, 580.

Hansard (1921). Vol. 138, Feb.–March 1921, Col. 1199.

Hanson, D.G. (1972). Welfare before the welfare state. In *The Long Debate on Poverty*, I.E.A. Readings, No. 9. IEA, London.

Harris, J. (1972). *Unemployment and Politics 1886–1914.* Oxford University Press, Oxford.

Harris, J. (1977). *William Beveridge: A Biography.* Oxford University Press, Oxford.

Harrison, M.L. (ed.) (1984). *Corporatism and the Welfare State.* Gower, Aldershot.

Harrison, M.L. (1986). Consumption and urban theory: An alternative approach based on the social division of welfare. *International Journal of Urban and Regional Research*, 10 (2): 232–42.

Harrison, R.J. and Zeitlin, J. (eds) (1985). *Divisions of Labour: Skilled Workers and Technological Change in Nineteenth Century England.* Harvester, Brighton.

Hay, J.R. (1975) *Origins of the Liberal Welfare Reforms 1906–1914.* Macmillan, London.

Hay, J.R. (1977). Employers and social policy in Britain: The evolution of welfare legislation, 1905–1914. *Social History*, 4: 435–55.

Heath, A. and McDonald, S.K. (1989). Social change and the future of the Left. In McDowell, L., Sarre, P. and Hamnett, C. (eds), *Divided Nation: Social and Cultural Change in Britain.* Hodder and Stoughton, London.

Henriques, U. (1979). *Before the Welfare State; Social Administration in Early Industrial Britain.* Longman, London.

Hills, J. (1987). What happened to spending on the welfare state? In Walker, A. and Walker, C. (eds), *The Growing Divide: A Social Audit 1979–87.* CPAG, London.

Himmelfarb, G. (1984). *The Idea of Poverty.* Faber and Faber, London.

Hindess, B. (1982). Power, interests and the outcomes of struggles. *Sociology*, 16 (4): 498–511.

Hinton, J. (1983). *Labour and Socialism 1867–1974.* Wheatsheaf, Brighton.

Hobsbawm, E.J. (1959). *Primitive Rebels: Studies in Archaic Forms of Social Movement in the 19th and 20th Centuries.* Manchester University Press, Manchester.

Hobsbawm, E.J. (1968). *Labouring Men.* Weidenfeld and Nicholson, London.

Holloway, J. and Picciotto, S. (eds) (1978). *State and Capital: A Marxist Debate.* Arnold, London.

Humphries, J. (1983). The emancipation of women in the 1970s and 1980s: From the latent to the floating. *Capital and Class*, 20: 6–28.

Hunt, E.H. (1981). *British Labour History 1815–1914.* Weidenfeld and Nicholson, London.

Inland Revenue (1990). Cmnd 1021, Chapter 21. HMSO, London.

Jessop, B. (1979). Corporatism, parliamentarism and social democracy. In Schmitter, P.C. and Lehmbruch, G. (eds), *Trends Toward Corporatist Intermediation.* Sage, London.

Johnson, N. (1987). *The Welfare State in Transition: The Theory and Practice of Welfare Pluralism.* Wheatsheaf, Brighton.

Jones, C. (1983). *State Social Work and the Working Class.* Macmillan, London.

Jordan, B. (1973). *Paupers: The Making of the Claiming Class*. Routledge and Kegan Paul, London.

Kaye, H.J. (1984). *The British Marxist Historians: An Introductory Analysis*. Polity, Cambridge.

Kelly, J. (1988). *Trade Unions and Socialist Politics*. Verso, London.

Kincaid, J. (1984). Richard Titmuss. In Barker, P. (ed.), *Founders of the Welfare State*. Heinemann, London.

Kingsford, P. (1982). *The Hunger Marchers in Britain, 1920–39*. Lawrence and Wishart, London.

Knights, D. and Wilmott, H. (eds) (1986a). *Gender and the Labour Process*. Gower, Aldershot.

Knights, D. and Wilmott, D. (eds) (1986b). *Managing the Labour Process*. Gower, Aldershot.

Knott, J. (1986). *Popular Opposition to the 1834 Poor Law*. Croom Helm, London.

Korpi, W. (1978). *The Working Class in Welfare Capitalism: Work Unions and Politics in Sweden*. Routledge and Kegan Paul, London.

Langan, M. (1985). Reorganizing the labour market: Unemployment, the state and the labour market. In Langan, M. and Schwarz, B. (eds), *Crises in the British State 1880–1930*. Hutchinson/CCCS, London/Birmingham.

Langan, M. and Schwarz, B. (eds) (1985). *Crises in the British State 1880–1930*. Hutchinson/CCCS, London/Birmingham.

Layton-Henry, Z. and Rich, P.B. (eds) (1986). *Race, Government and Politics in Britain*. Macmillan, London.

Leadbeater, C. (1987). Unions go to Marxism. *Marxism Today*, September, 22–7.

Leadbeater, C. (1989). In the land of the dispossessed. In McDowell, L., Sarre, P. and Hamnett, C. (eds), *Divided Nation: Social and Cultural Change in Britain*. Hodder and Stoughton, London.

Lee, P. and Raban, C. (1988). *Welfare Theory and Social Policy: Reform or Revolution?* Sage, London.

Leeson, R.A. (1980). *Travelling Brothers*. Granada, St. Albans.

Le Grand, J. (1982). *The Strategy of Equality*. Allen and Unwin, London.

Le Grand, J. (1987). The middle class use of the British social services. In Goodin, R.E. and Le Grand, J. (eds), *Not Only the Poor*. Allen and Unwin, London.

Le Grand, J. and Robinson, R. (eds) (1984). *Privatisation and the Welfare State*. Allen and Unwin, London.

Lewenhak, S. (1977). *Women and Trade Unions*. Benn, London.

Lewis, J. (1986). *Labour and Love: Women's Experience of Home and Family 1850–1940*. Basil Blackwell, Oxford.

Lewis, J. and Piachaud, D. (1987). Women and poverty in the twentieth century. In Glendinning, C. and Millar, J. (eds), *Women and Poverty in Britain*. Wheatsheaf, Brighton.

Liddington, J. and Norris, J. (1978). *One Hand Tied Behind Us: The Rise of the Women's Suffrage Movement*. Virago, London.

Littler, C.R. (1982). *The Development of the Labour Process in Capialist Societies: A Comparative Study of the Transformation of Work Organisation in Britain, Japan and the U.S.A.* Heinemann, London.

Littler, C.R. (ed.) (1985). *The Experience of Work*. Gower, Aldershot.

Lodge, D. (1988). *Nice Work*. Penguin, Harmondsworth.

Lonsdale, S. (1985). *Work and Inequality*. Longman, London.

Lonsdale, S. (1987). Patterns of paid work. In Glendinning, C. and Millar, J. (eds), *Women and Poverty in Britain*. Wheatsheaf, Brighton.

Lowe, R. (1986). *Adjusting to Democracy: The Role of the Ministry of Labour in British Politics, 1916–1939*. Clarendon Press, Oxford.

Lukes, S. (1974). *Power: A Radical View*. Macmillan, London.

Lynes, T. (1976). Unemployment Assistance Tribunals in the 1930s. In Adler, M. and Bradley, A. (eds), *Justice, Discretion and Poverty*. Professional Books, Oxon.

MacGregor, S. (1981). *The Politics of Poverty*. Longman, London.

MacNicol, J. (1987). In pursuit of the underclass. *Journal of Social Policy*, 16 (3): 293–318.

Mandel, E. (1978). *Late Capitalism*. New Left Books, London.

Mann, K. (1984). Incorporation, exclusion, underclasses and the unemployed. In Harrison, M. L. (ed.), *Corporatism and the Welfare State*. Gower, Aldershot.

Mann, K. (1986). The making of a claiming class – the neglect of agency in analyses of the Welfare State. *Critical Social Policy*, 15: 62–74.

Mann, K. and Anstee, J. (1989). *Growing Fringes: Hypothesis on the Development of Occupational Welfare*. Armley, Leeds.

Marwick, A. (1968). *Britain in the Century of Total War*. Bodley Head, London.

Marx, K. (1976). *Capital*. New Left Books/Penguin, London/Harmondsworth.

Marx, K. (1979). *Early Texts* (edited and translated by D. McLennan). Basil Blackwell, Oxford.

Marx, K. and Engels, F. (1956). *Selected Correspondence*. Lawrence and Wishart, London.

Marx, K. and Engels, F. (1969). *Basic Writings on Politics and Philosophy* (edited by L.S. Feuer). Collins/Fontana, London.

Marx, K. and Engels, F. (1971). *Articles on Britain*. Progress Publishers, Moscow .

Marx, K. and Engels, F. (1977). *The German Ideology* (edited by C.J. Arthur). Lawrence and Wishart, London.

Massey, D. (1984). *Spatial Divisions of Labour: Social Structures and the Geography of Production*. Macmillan, London.

McDowell, L., Sarre, P. and Hamnett, C. (eds) (1989). *Divided Nation: Social and Cultural Change in Britain*. Hodder and Stoughton, London.

McGoldrick, A. (1984). *Equal Treatment in Occupational Pension Schemes*. Equal Opportunities Commission, London.

McLoughlin, I. and Clark, J. (1988). *Technological Change at Work*. Open University Press, Milton Keynes.

Middlemas, K. (1979). *Politics in Industrial Society since 1911*. Andre Deutsch, London.

Middlemas, K. (1986). *Power, Competition and the State*. Macmillan, London.

Middleton, C. (1979). The sexual division of labour in feudal England. *New Left Review*, 113–114: 147–68.

Middleton, C. (1985). Women's labour and the transition to pre-industrial capitalism. In Charles, L. and Duffin, L. (eds), *Women and Work in Pre-Industrial England*. Croom Helm, London.

Middleton, L. (ed.) (1977). *Women in the Labour Movement*. Croom Helm, London.

Miles, R. (1989). Racism and class structure. In McDowell, L., Sarre, P. and Hamnett, C. (eds), *Divided Nation: Social and Cultural Change in Britain*. Hodder and Stoughton, London.

Miliband, R. (1973). *The State in Capitalist Society*. Quartet Books, London.

Miliband, R. (1974). Politics and poverty. In Wedderburn, D. (ed.), *Poverty, Inequality and Class Structure*. Cambridge University Press, Cambridge.

Mishra, R. (1984). *The Welfare State in Crisis: Social Thought and Social Change*. Wheatsheaf, Brighton.

Moorhouse, H.F. (1978). Marxist theories of the labour aristocracy. *Social History*, 3: 61–82.

Morris Committee (1929). Minutes of Evidence, Second Day, para.763.

Murphy, J.T. (1972). *Preparing for Power*. Cape, London.

Murphy, R. (1988). *Social Closure: The Theory of Monopolization and Exclusion*. Clarendon Press, Oxford.

Murray, C. (1990). *The Emerging British UNDERCLASS*. IEA Health and Welfare Unit, London

Musson, A.E. (1976). Class struggle and the labour aristrocracy. *Social History*, III: 335–56.

Newman, O. (1981). *The Challenge of Corporatism*. Macmillan, London.

Nottingham, C. (1986). Recasting bourgeois Britain? The British State in the years which followed the First World War. *International Review of Social History*, xxxi (3): 227–47.

Novak, T. (1988). *Poverty and the State: An Historical Sociology*. Open University Press, Milton Keynes.

O'Connor, J. (1973). *The Fiscal Crisis of the State*. St Martins Press, New York.

Offe, C. (1981). The attribution of public status to interest groups: Observations on the West German case. In Berger, S. (ed.), *Organising Interests in Western Europe*. Cambridge University Press, Cambridge.

Offe, C. (1982). Some contradictions of the modern welfare state. *Critical Social Policy*, 12 (2): 7–16

Offe, C. (1984). *Contradictions of the Welfare State* (edited by J. Keane). Hutchinson, London.

Ollman, B. (1976). *Alienation: Marx's Conception of Man in Capitalist Society*. Cambridge University Press, Cambridge.

Orwell, G. (1970). *Collected Essays, Journalism and Letters*. Penguin, Harmondsworth.

O'Tuathaigh, M.A.G. (1985). The Irish in nineteenth century Britain: Problems of integration. In Swift, R. and Gilley, S. (eds), *The Irish in the Victorian City*. Croom Helm, London.

Pahl, R. (1970). *Patterns of Urban Life*. Longman, London.

Pahl, R. (1975). *Whose City*. Penguin, Harmondsworth.

Pahl, R. (1984). *Divisions of Labour*. Basil Blackwell, Oxford.

Panitch, L. (1981). The limits of corporatism: Trade unions in the capitalist state. *New Left Review*, 125: 21–43.

Parkin, F. (1979). *Marxism and Class Theory: A Bourgeois Critique*. Tavistock, London.

Pearson, G. (1983). *Hooligan – A History of Respectable Fears*. Macmillan, London.

Pelling, H. (1958). *The British Communist Party*. Black, London.

Pelling, H. (1965). *The Origins of the Labour Party 1880–1900*. Clarendon Press, Oxford.

Pelling, H. (1968). *Popular Politics and Society in Late Victorian Britain*. Macmillan, London.

Phizalklea, A. (1983). *One Way Ticket Migration and Female Labour*. Routledge and Kegan Paul, London.

Piachaud, D. (1987a). The growth of poverty. In Walker, A. and Walker, C. (eds), *The Growing Divide: A Social Audit 1979–1987*. CPAG, London.

Piachaud, D. (1987b). Problems in the definition and measurement of poverty. *Journal of Social Policy*, 16 (2): 147–64.

Pimlott, B. (1977). *Labour and the Left in the 1930s*. Cambridge University Press, Cambridge.

Piore, M. and Sabel, C. (1984). *The Seond Industrial Divide: Possibilities for Prosperity*. Basic Books, New York.

Piven, F.F. and Cloward, R.A. (1977). *Poor People's Movements*. Pantheon, New York.

Piven, F.F. and Cloward, R. (1982). *The New Class War: Reagan's Attack on the Welfare State and its Consequences*. Pantheon, New York.

Pond, C., Field, F. and Winyard, S. (1976). Trade unions and taxation. *Studies for Trade Unionists*, 2 (6).

Pope, R., Pratt, A. and Hoyle, B. (eds) (1986). *Social Welfare in Britain 1885–1985*. Croom Helm, London.

Poster, M. (1984). *Foucault, Marxism and History: Mode of Production vs Mode of Information*. Polity, Cambridge.

Potter, S. (1986). Car tax concessions: Perk or problem. *Town and Country Planning*, 55 (6): 169–70.

Preteceille, E. (1986). Collective consumption, urban segregation, and social classes. *Environment and Planning, Society and Space*, 4: 145–54.

Preteceille, E. and Terrail, J.P. (1985). *Capitalism, Consumption and Needs* (translated by S. Mathews). Basil Blackwell, Oxford.

Price, R. and Bain, G.S. (1983). Union growth; dimensions, determinants and destiny. In Bain, G.S. (ed.), *Industrial Relations in Britain*. Basil Blackwell, Oxford.

Priestley, J.B. (1934). *English Journey*. Heinemann, London.

Prosser, T. (1981). The politics of discretion: Aspects of discretionary power in the supplementary benefits scheme. In Adler, M. and Asquith, S. (eds), *Discretion and Welfare*. Heinemann, London.

Ramdin, R. (1987). *The Making of the Black Working Class in Britain*. Gower, Aldershot.

Reddin, M. (1982). Occupation, welfare and social division. In Jones, C. and Stevenson, J. (eds), *The Year Book of Social Policy in Britain 1980–81*. Routledge and Kegan Paul, London.

Redmayne, R. (1950). *Ideals in Industry*. Petty and Sons, Leeds.

Rex, J. (1971). The concept of housing classes and the sociology of race relations. *Race*, 12: 293–301.

Rex, J. (1973). *Race, Colonialism and the City*. Routledge and Kegan Paul, London.

Rex, J. and Moore, J. (1967). *Race, Community and Conflict*. Oxford University Press, Oxford.

Rex, J. and Tomlinson, S. (1979). *Colonial Immigrants in a British City: A Class Analysis*. Routledge and Kegan Paul, London

Richter, D.C. (1981). *Riotous Victorians*. Ohio University Press, London.

Rose, H. (1981). Rereading Titmuss: The sexual division of welfare. *Journal of Social Policy*, 10 (4): 477–502.

Rowbotham, S. (1973). *Hidden from History*. Pluto Press, London.

Rude, G. (1980). *Ideology and Popular Protest*. Lawrence and Wishart, London.

Ryan, P. (1978). Poplarism 1894–1930. In Thane, P. (ed.), *The Origins of British Social Policy*. Croom Helm, London.

Sabel, C.F. (1982). *Work and Politics – The Division of Labour in Industry*. Cambridge University Press, Cambridge.

Sandford, C., Pond, C. and Walker, R. (eds) (1980). *Taxation and Social Policy*. Heinemann, London.

Saunders, P. (1981). *Social Theory and the Urban Question*. Hutchinson, London.

Saunders, P. (1986). Comment on Dunleavy and Preteceille. *Environment and Planning, Society and Space*, 4: 155–63.

Saunders, P. and Harris, C. (1990). Privatisation and the consumer. *Sociology*, 24 (1): 57–74.

Saville, J. (1975). The welfare state: An historical approach. In Butterworth, E. and Holman, R. (eds), *Social Welfare in Modern Britain*. Fontana/Collins, Glasgow.

Seccombe, W. (1986). Patriarchy stabilized: The construction of the male breadwinner wage norm in 19th century Britain. *Social History*, 11 (1): 53–80.

Shaw, C. (1987). Eliminating the yahoo, eugenics, Social Darwinism and Five Fabians. *History of Political Thought*, VIII (3): 521–44.

Sherman, M. (1985). 'It is not a case of numbers': A case study of institutional racism, 1941–1943. In Lunn, K. (ed.), *Race and Labour in Twentieth Century Britain*. Frank Cass, London.

Sinfield, A. (1978). Analyses in the social division of welfare. *Journal of Social Policy*, 7 (2): 129–56.

Sinfield, A. (1981). *What Unemployment Means*. Martin Robertson, Oxford.

Sinfield, A. (1986). Poverty, privilege and welfare. In Bean, P. and Whyne, D. (eds), *Barabara Wooton: Essays in Her Honour*. Tavistock, London.

Sivanandan, A. (1982). *A Different Hunger: Writings on Black Resistance*. Pluto Press, London.

Sked, A. and Cook, C. (1979). *Post-War Britain: A Political History*. Penguin, Harmondsworth.

Smith, D. (1982). *Conflict and Compromise*. Routledge and Kegan Paul, London.

Smith, D.J. (1977). *Racial Disadvantage in Britain – the PEP Report*. Penguin, Harmondsworth.

Smith, G. (1987). *When Jim Crow Met John Bull: Black American Soldiers in W.W. 2 Britain*. I.B. Tauris, London.

Social Trends (1983). Vol. 13. HMSO, London.

Social Trends (1986). Vol. 16. HMSO, London.

Social Trends (1987). Vol. 17. HMSO, London.

Social Trends (1988). Vol. 18. HMSO, London.

Social Trends (1991). Vol. 21. HMSO, London.

Soldon, N.C. (1978). *Women in British Trade Unions, 1874–1976*. Gill and Macmillan, Dublin.

Stark, D. (1982). Class struggle and the transformation of the labour process. In Giddens, A. and Held, D. (eds), *Classes, Power, and Conflict: Classical and Contemporary Debates*. Macmillan, London.

Stedman-Jones, G. (1983). *Languages of Class*. Cambridge University Press, Cambridge.

Stedman-Jones, G. (1984). *Outcast London*. Oxford University Press, Oxford.

Stevenson, J. (1977). *Social Conditions in Britain between the Wars*. Penguin, Harmondsworth.

Stevenson, J. and Cook, C. (1977). *The Slump: Society and Politics During the Depression*. Jonathan Cape, London.

Swift, I. and Gilley, R. (eds) (1985). *The Irish in the Victorian City*. Croom Helm, London.

Taylor, B. (1983). The men are as bad as their masters. In Newton, J.L., Ryan, M.P. and Walkowitzt, J.R. (eds), *Sex and Class in Women's History*. Routledge and Kegan Paul, London.

Taylor-Gooby, P. (1981). The empiricist tradition in social adminstration. *Critical Social Policy*, 1 (2): 6–21.

Taylor-Gooby, P. (1985). *Public Opinion, Ideology and State Welfare*. Routledge and Kegan Paul, London.

Thane, P. (1975). The working class and state welfare 1880–1914. *Society for the Study of Labour History*. Bulletin 31.

Thane, P. (1978). *The Origins of British Social Policy*. Croom Helm, London.

Thane, P. (1982). *Foundations of the Welfare State*. Longman, London.

Thane, P. (1984). The working class and state welfare in Britain, 1880–1914. *The Historical Journal*, **27** (4): 877–900.

Therborn, G. (1983). Why some classes are more successful than others. *New Left Review*, **138**: 37–56.

Thomis, M.I. (1976). *Responses to Industrialisation: The British Experience 1780–1850*. David and Charles, Newton Abbot.

Thompson, E.P. (1968). *The Making of the English Working Class*. Penguin, Harmondsworth.

Thompson, E.P. (1978). Peculiarities of the English. In *The Poverty of Theory and other Essays*. Merlin, London.

Thompson, E.P. (1980). *Writing by Candlelight*. Merlin, London.

Thompson, E.P. (1984). Mr Attlee and the Gadarene Swine. *The Guardian*, 3 March.

Titmuss, R.M. (1958). *Essays on the Welfare State*. Allen and Unwin, London.

Titmuss, R.M. (1959). *The Irresponsible Society*. Fabian Society, London.

Titmuss, R.M. (1962). *Income Distribution and Social Change: A Study in Criticism*. Allen and Unwin, London.

Titmuss, R.M. (1970). *The Gift Relationship – From Human Blood to Social Policy*. Allen and Unwin, London.

Townsend, P. (1979). *Poverty in the United Kingdom*. Penguin, Harmondsworth.

Townsend, P. (1987). Poor health. In Walker, A. and Walker, C. (eds), *The Growing Divide: A Social Audit 1979–87*. CPAG, London.

Treble, J.H. (1968). The Place of Irish Catholics in the Social Life of the North of England 1829–51. Unpublished PhD thesis, University of Leeds.

Treble, J.H. (1979). *Urban Poverty in Britain, 1830–1914*. Batsford, London.

Trotsky, L. (1975). *The Struggle Against Fascism in Germany*. Penguin, Harmondsworth.

Walby, S. (1986). *Patriarchy at Work: Patriarchal and Captalist Relations in Employment*. Polity, Cambridge.

Walby, S. (1990). *Theorizing Patriarchy*. Basil Blackwell, Oxford.

Walker, A. (1984). The political economy of privatisation. In Le Grand, J. and Robinson, R. (eds), *Privatisation and the Welfare State*. George Allen and Unwin, London.

Walker, A. and Walker, C. (eds) (1987). *The Growing Divide: A Social Audit 1979–1987*. CPAG, London.

Walker, R. and Lawton, D. (1989). Social assistance and territorial justice: The example of single payments. *Journal of Social Policy*, **17** (4): 437–76.

Ward, J.T. and Fraser, H. (1980). *Workers and Employers: Documents on Trade Union and Industrial Relations in Britain since the 18th Century*. Macmillan, London.

Ward, S. (1981). *Pensions*. Pluto Press, London

Ward, S. (1985). The financial crisis facing pensioners. *Critical Social Policy*, **14**: 43–56.

Warde, A. (1990). Introduction to the sociolgy of consumption. *Sociology*, **24** (1): 1–4.

Webb, B. and Webb, S. (1916). *The Prevention of Destitution*. Longman, London.

Webb, B. and Webb, S. (1920). *History of Trade Unionism*. Longman, London.

Weber, M. (1968). *Economy and Society*. Bedminster Press, New York.

Wetherly, P. (1988). Class struggle and the welfare state: Some theoretical problems considered. *Critical Social Policy*, **22**: 24–40.

White, J. (1982). 1910–1914 reconsidered. In Cronin, J.G. and Schneer, J. (eds), *Social Conflict and the Political Order in Modern Britain*. Croom Helm, London.

Whitehead, M. (1987). *The Health Divide: Inequalities in Health in the 1980s*. Health Education Council, London.

Whiteside, N. (1980). Welfare and the unions in the First World War. *The Historical Journal*, **23** (4): 857–74.

Wilensky, H.L. (1976). *The New Corporatism, Centralization and the Welfare State*. Sage, London.

Wilkinson, F. (ed.) (1981). *The Dynamics of Labour Market Segmentation*. Academic Press, London.

Williams, N.J., Sewel, J.F. and Twine, F. (1986). Council house sales and residualisation. *Journal of Social Policy*, **15** (3): 273–92.

Willman, P. (1986). *Technological Change, Collective Bargaining and Industrial Efficiency*. Oxford University Press, Oxford.

Wilson, E. (1977). *Women and the Welfare State*. Tavistock, London.

Wilson, H. (1974). *The Labour Government 1964–70*. Penguin, Harmondsworth.

Wilson, W.J. (1987). *The Truly Disadvantaged: The Inner City, The Underclass and Public Policy*. University of Chicago Press, Chicago.

Wilson, W.J. (ed.) (1987). *The Ghetto Underclass*. Special edition of the Annals of the American Academy of Political and Social Science. Sage, London.

Winyard, S. (1987). Divided Britain. In Walker, A. and Walker, C. (eds), *The Growing Divide: A Social Audit 1979–1987*. CPAG, Bath.

Wook, S. and Windolph, P. (1987). *Social Closure in the Labour Market*. Gower, Aldershot.

Wraithe, R.E. and Hutcheson, P. (1973). *Administrative Tribunals*. Allen and Unwin, London.

Wright, S. (1985). Churmaids, Huswyfes and Hucksters. In Charles, L. and Duffin, L. (eds), *Women and Work in Pre-Industrial England*. Croom Helm, London.

Yeo, S. (1979). Working class associations, private capital, welfare and the state in the late nineteenth and twentieth centuries. In Parry, N., Rustin, M. and Satyamurti, C. (eds), *Social Work, Welfare and the State*. Arnold, London.

Index

Abercrombie, N., 44–5
actuarial principles, 47, 60, 97, 155
  see also insurance principles
administration
  pressure upon, 70–3
  working class involvement in, 40,
    51–4, 64–7, 70–2
AEU/ASE/AUEW, 3, 59, 77, 86, 162
agency, 135–6, 144
Aglietta, M., 120
Alexander, S., 37
alienation, 10–11, 19, 148, 152–6, 158,
  163
Anderson, P., 41, 44
Andrzejewski, S., 73
anomie, 14–15, 163
apprenticeships, 29, 35, 46–7, 150
Armstrong, P., 157–8
artisans, 33, 139–40
Asian workers, 89
Atkinson, J., 120
Australia, 53, 56

Bagguley, P., 120
Barbalet, J., 128
Barnett, S., 51
Barron, R., 119
Belchem, J., 38
Belfast, 37
Bentham, J., 40
Best, G., 44
Bevan, A., 87
Beveridge, W., 12, 51, 53, 74–8, 81
Bevin, E., 77
Blackburn, R., 121

Booth, C., 12, 46, 50–1
Booth, W., 48
Bovenkerk, F., 132
Bowles, S., 135
Braverman, H., 4, 7, 18–20, 63–4, 135
Braybon, G., 59, 77
Briggs, A., 71
Building Societies, 87, 95, 103, 117,
  152
building trade, workers in, 37
Burgess, K., 56
Byrne, D., 145–7

car
  company cars, 94–5, 98, 107
  industry, 83, 99
carpenters, 41
Castells, M., 113
Castle, B., 91
Castles, S., 135
Catholics, 38
Chadwick, E., 12
Chamberlain, J., 51, 53
Charles, L., 29
Chartism, 38, 40–2, 45
chemical industry, 83
Churchill, W., 53–4, 63
claimants, 100, 109–10, 162
Claimants Unions, 3, 91–2, 141
class consciousness, 44–6, 51, 140–1,
  159
class struggle, 27, 79, 108, 123, 144–8
  passim, 164
  and the labour process, 7, 157–9
  and Marxist theory, 22, 135–6

closed shop agreements, 81
Clydeside, 66
Clynes, J., 65
colour bar, the, 77, 87
communications industry, 98
Communist Party, 72, 76, 79, 114–15
consensus, 77, 80
conservatism within working class, 42,
    73, 133, 140
Conservative Government, 13, 97, 114,
    128, 161
consumption, 10, 102–3, 105, 110–19,
    142–6, 161–5 passim
  cleavages, 10, 98, 112, 116–17, 129
  collective, 111–18
Cook, D., 163
Cooperative Societies, 41, 45, 152
core and peripheral workers, 91,
    119–20
  see also flexibility
corporatism, 9, 74–81 passim, 86,
    91–3, 162
Corrigan, P., 133
Cossick, G., 44
council housing, 68, 70, 100–2,
    109–12, 114
  see also housing
Courts of Referees, 64–5
crime, 50, 106
criminals, 50, 130–2, 138
Cripps, S., 83
Cronin, J., 68–9, 77
Crouch, C., 75
Crowther, M., 40–1, 44

Deacon, A., 65–6, 71, 81
debt, 117
  see also mortgage arrears
demarcation, 82
  see also restrictive practices
dependence, 14–17, 19, 148–52, 154,
    158, 164
  see also needs
deserving, 21, 30
  and undeserving distinction, 40,
    49–50, 54–7, 64, 67
DHSS, 92, 136
  see also social security
dilution of labour, 36, 62
discrimination, 57, 118–20, 123, 129,
    137, 159
  housing and, 108–9
  Irish and, 38–40

racial, 88
women and, 97
distributive networks, 108, 110, 115
diswelfare, 25, 151
division of labour, 7, 13–17, 20, 31,
    138–9, 149
dockers, 49, 59, 84–5, 88
'dodgers', 76
Donnison, D., 12
'dossers', 3, 93
dual closure, 10, 46, 89, 125–8, 159–61
    passim, 164
dual labour market theory, 10, 91,
    118–24, 129, 137
Dublin, 37
Dunleavy, P., 111–12, 116
Durkheim, E., 14–17, 24

economism, 42–8 passim, 78, 84, 140,
    152, 159
education, 104, 109–11, 123–4, 127
Edwards, R., 156, 158
electricity
  industry, 98
Engels, F., 131–2
engineering, 7, 41, 43, 59, 61, 68
  industry, 83, 99
  Unions, 3
  see also AEU, ASE, AUEW
Equal Opportunities Commission
    (EOC), 97
equal pay, 59, 77, 91
Essex, 114
exclusion, 47, 73, 136–7, 147–55
    passim, 159–65 passim
  from consumption patterns, 115, 144
  from corporatism, 86
  from Guilds and Friendly Societies,
    30–7
  as a form of social closure, 46,
    124–9, 159–60, 164–5
  from trade unions, 89, 140–2
  of women, 65–6, 77, 91–3

false consciousness, 159
family wage, 37, 77
feminism, 24, 56, 135
Fenians, 42
Field, F., 2
fiscal welfare, 10, 21, 33, 93–7, 103,
    159–65 passim
  neglect of, 118–19
  sexual divisions and, 25–6

Titmuss's account of, 5, 7, 15–16, 68
   see also taxation
Fitzgerald, R., 69
flexibility/flexible working, 99–100,
   119–20
Flynn, R., 101
Forrest, R. 101
Foster, J., 42–3
Fox, A., 69
Fraser, D., 44
Friend, A., 145, 147
Friendly Societies, 39–47 *passim*, 60,
   66, 116–17, 150–2 *passim*, 163
   before 1800, 30–3
   and the Liberal reforms, 50–7 *passim*
   and TUCs evidence to Beveridge
      Committee, 76
fringe benefits, 119, 122–3
   see also occupational welfare
Fryer, P., 88–9
full employment, 74–5, 80–3, 85
funeral grants, 41

Galbraith, K., 116
gas
   industry, 98
   workers, 49
general unionism, 49
Genuinely Seeking Work Test (GSWT),
   64–7, 78
Germany, 52, 56, 69, 83
Giddens, A., 2, 87
Ginsburg, N., 53–4, 134, 136
Gintis, H., 135
Goldthorpe, J., 116
Gosden, P., 32, 39, 47
Gough, I., 2, 75
Gray, R., 45
Green, F., 99, 122–3
guilds, 28–31, 33–5

Halevy, E., 51–2
Hannah, L., 70
harmonization, 99–100
Harris, J., 51–3, 76
Harrison, M., 146
Hay, J., 52, 55–6
Hayday, A., 66–7, 92
health, 102, 110, 115, 152
Heath, E., 86
Hindess, B., 159
Hinton, J., 45, 82
Hobsbawm, E., 30, 34, 43

holidays as benefits, 69–70, 98, 100,
   109
homeless, the, 92
housing, 5–6, 89, 95–102 *passim*,
   108–16 *passim*, 145, 151–5 *passim*
housing classes, 10, 87, 105, 108–9,
   129, 160
Hyndman, H., 49–50

immigrants, 31, 33, 37, 88, 134–5
immigration, 50, 87–9, 126
imperialism, 42, 48
incomes policies, 81, 86
incorporation of organized labour, 82,
   125
independent labourers, 39–41
India, 87
industrialization, 14, 17–20, 27, 150
insurance
   National, 40, 53–6, 59–61, 64–7
   principles, 40, 79
Irish, the, 50, 57, 88, 148, 160
   exclusion of, 31, 137, 150–1
   strike breakers, 37–8

Japan, 83
Jarrow, 67
Jessop, B., 2, 82
Jews, exclusion of, 50, 57, 88, 137,
   148, 160

Kaye, H., 4
Kosack, G., 135

labour aristocracy, 42–9 *passim*, 76–82
   passim, 116, 126, 140, 155–8
   passim
labour colonies, 51
labour exchanges, 31, 52
Labour Governments, 75, 89, 93
labour market, theories of
   orthodox, 118
   see also dual labour market theory
Labour Party, 50, 65–6, 72–3, 79, 89,
   161–2
labour process, 4, 27, 57, 70, 76,
   163–4
   alienation and, 18–20, 152–9
   consumption and, 145–6
   contests for control over, 7–9, 34–5,
      63–4
   divisive effects of, 11, 47–8, 59, 137,
      148–9

flexible working and, 99
labour aristocracy and, 42
labour market and, 78–85 *passim*,
104
labour specifity, 14, 18, 20
labourism, 73
lapilli, 160–1
Leeds, 69
legitimation, 21
Le Grand, J., 94
Leninism, 130–1
Leonard, P., 133
Liberal reforms, 9, 40, 52–6
life chances, 108–9, 114–15, 124, 127,
129
Liverpool, 59, 114
Lloyd-George, D., 55–6, 62–3
Local Employment Committees (LEC),
65, 70–2, 92
Loch, C., 51
Lockwood, D., 116
London, 36–7, 46, 50, 68, 133, 139–40
Lukes, S., 151
lumpen-proletariat, 10, 50, 131–3, 146,
160

Macdonald, R., 50, 66
MacGregor, S., 76
Malthus, T., 40
Manchester, 64
Manchester Unity of Oddfellows, 41,
55
Mann, M., 121
Mann, T., 49
marginalization, 2, 77–8, 133, 139–44
passim, 160, 163
Marshall, A., 51
Marx, K., 2, 7, 34, 46, 50, 116, 149–58
passim ·
Marxism, 24, 113, 123–5, 128, 151,
159
Massey, D., 145
Metcalf, A., 145, 147
middle classes
ideology and, 45–8, 55
as 'observers' of the poor, 38, 42–51
passim, 131–9 *passim*, 146–50
passim, 162–5
welfare benefits and, 13, 16, 47, 94,
107
Middlemas, K., 63, 67
Midlands, the, 68
Miliband, R., 141

miners, 122
mining, 36
industry, 83, 99
model unionism, 41
Moore, R., 109–10
moral
fibre undermined by welfare state, 13
hypocrisy and middle classes, 107
individualism, 14–15
regulation, need for, 15, 106, 131–2
mortgages, 6, 95, 97, 111, 144, 162–5
arrears, 103
motor manufacture, 76
see also car industry
Murie, A., 101
Murphy, R., 127–8
Murray, C., 1–2, 106–7, 128–9, 132

NALGO, 70
NCB, 122
needs, 14–17, 44, 149, 151–2
see also dependence
New Zealand, 56
NHS, 5, 14, 25, 104, 111, 162–3
Norris, G., 119
Novak, T., 136, 141
NUWM, 67, 72, 79, 141

occupational welfare, 9–10, 25, 118,
159, 161–5
dual labour market theory and, 91,
122–3
during 1920s and 30s, 68–70, 78, 86
recent developments, 94, 96–100
Titmuss' account of 5–7, 15–16
Offe, C., 142
Old Age Pensions Act 1908, 54–6
Oldham, 36
Orwell, G., 72, 74–5
O'Tuathaigh, M., 38
owner occupation, 95–7, 102–3, 107,
109, 128

Pakistanis, 87
Panitch, L., 82, 86
Parkin, F., 2, 35, 124–9, 137, 159–64
passim
dual closure, 10, 46, 64, 89
paternalism, 63, 68–9, 100
patriachy, 20, 26, 36, 134–9 *passim*,
148–52 *passim*, 160–4 *passim*
paupers, 39–41, 55, 116
pauperism, 32, 38–41, 55–6, 131, 138

Pelling, H., 43
pensions, 23, 86, 96–100, 110, 164
  1908 Act, 54–6
  funds, 95
  occupational/company, 6, 68–70, 96–9, 107, 120, 144
Piore, M., 120
police, the, 92–3, 101
Poor Law, 8, 38–41, 47–54 passim, 61, 66, 149–50
  consumption cleavages and, 116
  opposition to, 136, 141
  social divisions created by, 126, 128
Poplar, 51, 71
Post-Fordism, 119–20, 124, 129
  neglect of race and gender, 120
potters, 36
poverty, 23, 38, 46, 93, 150–8 passim
  vulnerability of working class and, 43, 57
  women and, 36–7, 144
Powell, E., 88
power, 97, 163
  powerlessness and, 70, 109, 151
  SDW and, 20–4 passim
  the state and, 126–8
pragmatic acceptance/pragmatism, 9, 41, 44–7, 112, 114, 155–62 passim
Preteceille, E., 113, 117
Priestley, J., 69
printing, and printers, 37, 158
privatization, 118
profit sharing schemes, 99–100, 144
Prosser, T., 71
Public Assistance Committees (PACs), 65, 70–2
public relief works, 51, 53
public welfare, 25–6, 33, 112, 118, 144, 162–5
  legitimation and, 21
  recent developments, 100–7 passim
  Sinfield's account of, 13, 95

racism, 3, 20, 48, 93, 139–41 passim, 160–4 passim
  housing and, 109
  immigration, response to, 87–9
  labour market and, 118
  during Second World War, 77–8
Ramdin, R., 89
reformism, 45, 140, 162

Relative Surplus/Stagnant Population (RSP), 131, 138–9, 160
Reserve Army of Labour (RAL), 2–3, 10, 61, 131–40, 146–7, 160
residualization, 101, 110–11, 147
residuum, 2, 78, 97, 104–11 passim, 160
  Marxism and, 133, 140, 146
  middle class observers and, 46, 51
respectability, 40, 44
respectable working class, 47–55 passim, 65, 93–5 passim, 107, 112, 140
restrictive practices, 7, 9, 19, 83–5, 157
Rex, J., 2, 88, 108–10, 115
'right to buy' legislation, 95, 101
'ring fencing', 89–90
riots, 41, 88, 93, 140–1
Rose, H., 24–5, 27, 37, 144
Rotherham, 71
'roughs' within working class, 38, 47, 49–50, 54, 111, 137
Rowbotham, S., 136
Rowntree, S., 12

Sabel, C., 120
Salvation Army, 51
Saunders, P., 109–17 passim, 142, 145
scientific management, 68–9, 90
'scroungers', 3, 65–6, 93
sectarianism, 72, 79
sectionalism, 16, 42–8 passim, 61–2, 90, 148–55 passim, 159–63 passim
self help, 31, 44, 116, 150, 155
sexism, 3, 93, 141
sexual divisions, 4, 25, 27, 29, 65, 151
  of labour, 20–8 passim, 32–9 passim, 58–9, 90–1, 119–21, 144
  of welfare, 24–6, 39
sexual harassment, 92, 151
share participation schemes, 99–100, 144
Shaw, C., 46
'shirkers', 65–6
shop stewards, 62, 76, 83, 85–6, 89, 161
sickness benefits/sick pay, 32, 69–70, 86, 98, 100, 150
Sinfield, A., 2, 26–7, 70, 94–7 passim, 111, 126
  revision of SDW thesis, 16–24 passim, 163
  social security classes and, 108–9

single parents, 91, 110, 114, 136,
    161–2
Smiles, S., 44, 116
Smithfield meat porters, 88
social closure, 35, 64, 105, 124–9, 137,
    148–50 passim
Social Darwinism, 46, 48, 50, 57, 132,
    139
Social Democratic Federation (SDF),
    49–50, 140
social reproduction, 142–6
    see also consumption
Social Security, 5, 102, 115
    classes, 105, 108, 129, 160
    see also DHSS
social welfare, 5, 7, 16
    see also public welfare
squatters/squatting, 92
State, the, 34, 85, 88, 143, 146–7, 150
    corporatism and, 75
    Friendly Societies and, 39, 54
    Murray's view of, 106
    Parkin's view of, 125–8
    structural accounts of, 3–4, 20–4
        passim, 111–13, 135–7
    Titmuss's view of, 13–15, 17, 73
Stedman-Jones, G., 2, 46, 132–3,
    139–40
strike breakers, 37, 147
Summerfield, P., 77
Sunderland, 102
syndicalism, 52, 56

tailoring, 37, 69
tailors, 36
taxation, 5–6, 53, 55, 82, 93–7, 112
    see also fiscal welfare
tax evasion, 21
taxonomies, 124
    and invention, 109–10, 115, 121, 139
Taylor, F., 63, 69
textiles industry, 36, 69, 83, 99
TGWU, 49, 86
Thane, P., 55–6, 73
Thatcher, M., 93
Therborn, G., 84–5, 158
Thompson, E., 4, 33–4, 43
thrift, 55
time, 20, 23
Titmuss, R., 33, 82, 103, 108, 127,
    146–53 passim, 158–65 passim
    consumption patterns and, 111, 116,
    118

impact of war, 73
needs and the SDW, 4–6
the SDW thesis, 12–27, 68, 70, 94, 105
Toynbee, A., 51
trades councils, 50, 64, 92, 141
tramping, 31, 33
transport, 94–5, 111
Treble, J., 38
TUC, 50–4 passim, 59–67 passim, 72–9
    passim, 83–90 passim, 115, 141

UAB, 71–2, 141
underclass(es), 1–2, 10, 46, 50, 87, 91,
    160–5 passim
    Murray's view of, 105–8
undeserving, 21, 50, 66–7
    see also deserving
unemployables, 78, 104, 107
unemployed, the, 31, 47, 52–3, 68,
    70–3
unemployment, 9–10, 101–4, 106–10
    passim, 150, 157, 161–4 passim
    in 19th century, 49, 51
    in inter-war period, 60–1, 66–8, 70–3
    in 1960s and 70s, 85–7, 93
    in 1980s, 23, 133
    Reserve Army of Labour and,
        133–41
USA, 69, 77, 83, 88, 106, 118–26
    passim

wages, 49, 68, 73, 81–3, 93–9 passim,
    122, 138
    differentials, 42–3, 159, 161
    women's, 59, 90
wage slavery, 149–52, 154
Walby, S., 144
Warde, A., 117
Webb, B., 12, 51, 61
Weber, M., 116, 124, 126
Weberian sociology, 20–4, 90, 105–10
    passim, 113–16 passim, 124–6
    passim, 142
welfare rights organizations, 91
West Indies/West Indians, 87, 89
Whiteside, N., 60–1
widows benefit, 32
Willman, P., 84
Wilson, H., 84–5
'women's libbers', 93
workhouses, 33, 37, 93, 150
    see also Poor Law
workpeoples' representatives, 64–7, 71